国家级一流本科课程配套教材

商务职场沟通英语

主　编　刘　畅
副主编　徐林林　邢　青
编　者　张林华　吕　汀
　　　　徐世红　俞　博

清华大学出版社
北京

内容简介

本教材分为八个单元，围绕职场环境中的典型交际行为与活动来介绍英语语言知识和交际技能，包括步入职场、业务联络、商务策划三大模块，涉及制作个人简历、准备求职面试、撰写工作邮件、参加商务接待、介绍公司情况、进行市场调查、参加工作会议、起草新产品提案等典型应用场景，既提供贴近真实职场环境的学习素材，又渗透中西方文化的对比，着重培养学生的英语综合表达能力、跨文化交际能力、混合式学习能力和批判性思维能力。本教材还有配套的慕课资源，教师可开展线上线下相结合的混合式教学实践。教材配套的教师资源、PPT课件、练习题参考答案等，读者可登录 www.tsinghuaelt.com 下载使用。

本教材适合高校非英语专业本科生使用，也可供有商务职场沟通需求的学习者参考使用。

版权所有，侵权必究。举报：010-62782989，beiqinquan@tup.tsinghua.edu.cn。

图书在版编目（CIP）数据

商务职场沟通英语 / 刘畅主编. — 北京：清华大学出版社，2023.5
国家级一流本科课程配套教材
ISBN 978-7-302-63539-0

Ⅰ. ①商⋯ Ⅱ. ①刘⋯ Ⅲ. ①商务—英语—高等学校—教材 Ⅳ. ①F7

中国国家版本馆 CIP 数据核字（2023）第 087054 号

责任编辑：刘　艳
封面设计：子　一
责任校对：王凤芝
责任印制：曹婉颖

出版发行：清华大学出版社
　　网　　址：http://www.tup.com.cn, http://www.wqbook.com
　　地　　址：北京清华大学学研大厦 A 座　　邮　编：100084
　　社 总 机：010-83470000　　邮　购：010-62786544
　　投稿与读者服务：010-62776969, c-service@tup.tsinghua.edu.cn
　　质量反馈：010-62772015, zhiliang@tup.tsinghua.edu.cn
印 装 者：北京嘉实印刷有限公司
经　　销：全国新华书店
开　　本：185mm×260mm　　印　张：13.25　　字　数：280 千字
版　　次：2023 年 6 月第 1 版　　印　次：2023 年 6 月第 1 次印刷
定　　价：56.00 元

产品编号：097429-01

前言

一、编写背景

党的二十大报告指出,"深入实施人才强国战略"需要"着力形成人才国际竞争的比较优势"。我国大学生国际竞争优势的形成离不开全球胜任力的培养,而跨文化沟通和交流能力是全球胜任力的核心素养。《商务职场沟通英语》服务于人才强国战略,着眼于提升大学生的全球胜任力素养,立足于提高大学生在参与国际商务事务中的英语理解与表达能力、分析与解决问题的能力、平等协商与沟通协作的能力、人文思辨能力和创新思维能力。

二、编写理念

本教材面向非英语专业本科学生,是一本专门用途英语(English for Specific Purposes)类教材。本教材充分体现《大学英语教学指南(2020版)》的精神,遵循"分类指导、因材施教"的原则,采用"循序渐进、进阶挑战"的设计理念,前六个单元针对"提高目标",后两个单元针对"发展目标",既支持各个学校根据校情、学情特点安排教学,也满足学生的个性化需求。

三、单元结构

本教材围绕若干商务和工作场景中的典型任务展开,涉及步入职场、业务联络、商务策划三大应用场景模块,每个场景分别包括一到两个写作项目或口语项目,所有八个项目构成了教材的八个单元,详见下表:

应用场景	写作项目	口语项目
模块一:步入职场	第一单元:制作个人简历	第二单元:准备求职面试
模块二:业务联络	第三单元:撰写工作邮件	第四单元:参加商务接待
		第五单元:介绍公司情况
模块三:商务策划	第七单元:进行市场调查	第六单元:参加工作会议
	第八单元:起草新产品提案	

每个单元均按照基于项目(project-based)的教学法来设计,具体的活动编排思路如下:

Knowing What	Section I　Warm-Up	引入话题和项目应用场景
	Section II　Pre-writing/Pre-speaking	明确概念和项目相关知识
Knowing How	Section III　Planning	规划产品和项目整体框架
	Section IV　Drafting/Practicing	制作产品和项目主体创作或训练
Knowing Why	Section V　Reflection	试验产品和项目效果反思
	Section VI　Exposition	展示作品和项目成果验收
	Section VII　Wrap-Up	评价收获和项目学习反思

四、主要特色

1. 理念先进，有效促学

本教材的活动设计融合了以学生为中心的"产出导向"（output-oriented）教学法，以输出驱动学习、以输入促成学习，达到以用促学、学用一体的效果。此外，教材根据"支架教学法"（Scaffolding）和"最近发展区"（Zone of Proximal Development）理论，为学生提供了详细的项目教学支架，并相当重视"问题产品"的反馈作用，通过单元内活动引导学生去观察、分析、修改"问题产品"的典型错误，从而提升学习效果。为检测学习效果，每个单元还提供了"形成性"（formative）测评量规，充分体现了"学—教—测"的统一。

2. 材料丰富，有趣实用

本教材的学习材料十分丰富，包括场景对话、阅读文本、精选视频、活动练习、解答示范、案例分析和评分量规等多种异质化、多模态的素材。教材选材紧密结合国际商务实务和职场交流实际。材料实用性强，便于学生理解和运用。同时，材料具有趣味性和启发性，有助于培养学生的中国情怀和国际视野。学习材料的内容前后续接、难度渐进，让项目任务具有一定的难易梯度和挑战性，便于学生开展个性化、进阶式的学习。

3. 慕课关联，轻松混合

本教材是国家级一流本科课程和国家精品在线开放课程的配套教材。学生登录"中国大学MOOC"在线学习平台，输入"职场沟通英语"课程名称，即可选课。本教材与慕课的进度大体同步，其内容既有交叉，又有区别。慕课内容高度概括，科普性强，适合学生自学入门；教材内容步步深入，有一定的挑战性，适合教师开展线下课堂教学。

在此，编者提供两种混合式学习模式供学生和授课教师参考。第一种模式：学生通过扫描教材中的二维码自主学习已提供的授课视频，并完成相关任务；教师在课堂上主要围绕未提供授课视频的活动展开教学。第二种模式：学生全程参与线上慕课的学习；教师在课堂上主要围绕产出难度大或需要小组合作的活动展开教学。

五、配套资源

为便于教师发挥教学主导作用，本教材还配有"口语传达方式的基本知识与技能""单元活动与书面沟通知识技能对照表""单元活动与口头沟通知识技能对照表""单元思政元素汇总表"以及参考答案、电子课件等相关资源，教师可登录"清华社英语在线"数字化互动教学平台获取。

六、编写团队

本教材的编写团队由电子科技大学长期从事大学英语教学的一线教师组成。团队教师教学经验丰富，获得多项国家级、省部级教学成果。

由于编者水平有限，教材中的遗漏和错误在所难免，诚挚希望广大读者对本教材提出宝贵的意见和建议，以便我们不断改进和完善。

编者
2023年2月

Contents

Module I   Embarking on a New Career 1

Unit 1   Writing a Resume 3
Unit 2   Handling a Job Interview 29

Module II   Making Business Connections 49

Unit 3   Writing an Email 51
Unit 4   Receiving Visitors 75
Unit 5   Giving a Presentation 95

Module III   Developing Strategies for a New Product 127

Unit 6   Attending Meetings 129
Unit 7   Conducting a Market Survey 153
Unit 8   Writing a New Product Proposal 179

Appendix 203

Module I

Embarking on a New Career

Unit 1
Writing a Resume

商务职场沟通英语

 **Section 1** *Warm-Up*

Activity ❶ Initiating the Unit

There are many things to do in a job application process. What do you know about those things?

Task: Choose a topic from the following two options and share your experience or plan with a partner or the class. Some useful expressions are offered in the box below. You can use them when you speak.

1) If you have a job now, talk about your experience in your last job seeking.

2) If you are going to apply for a job, talk about what you will do in your upcoming job-seeking journey.

write a resume	attend a job interview
send a cover letter	complete and submit an application form
go to graduate job fairs	read a job advertisement for a vacancy
work on probation	consult a career counselor
take a psychometric test	

Activity ❷ Understanding the Key Concept

Jim meets his roommate Chris in the dorm and asks him how his job hunting is going. Read the conversation in pairs and complete the task that follows.

Jim: Chris, some best companies will come to our campus next month. Do you know it?

Chris: Yes, I do. But I'm not in the mood. You know I'm still feeling down with my last

Unit 1 Writing a Resume

application.

Jim: Someone told you that you'd been turned town?

Chris: No. I haven't had any calls from them yet. I guess I didn't make it.

Jim: Don't worry, dude. You always do well at school. I'm sure your good grades will help you get a job soon.

Chris: Thanks, Jim. I hope so.

Jim: The only thing you need is a comprehensive **resume**. It can help you to win.

Chris: Absolutely! I'll revise it soon. Can you help me to polish it?

Jim: My pleasure. So, you owe me a meal.

Chris: That's a deal.

Task: Explain what a resume is in your own words.

_____

_____

You can check the reference here.

Knowledge Notes

A resume is a formal document that summarizes a job applicant's qualifications, including education-related and work-related experiences, skills, achievements, etc. It helps the job applicant to demonstrate qualities and convince employers to offer the position.

Section II *Pre-writing*

Activity 3 Giving Opinions on Photo Use

Read some reasons for or against photo use on resumes. Then discuss the following questions in groups and write down your answers.

1) What is your opinion about photo use on resumes?
2) Which of the following reasons do you support?

For:

1. Since your employer will see you face to face during the interview, a resume photo won't make any difference.
2. A professional-looking photo gives you a plus. In some companies or sectors, job applicants are supposed to offer a photo to meet the requirements. If you don't, they will reject you.
3. Different cultures see this issue differently. Using a photo on a resume may not always lead to offense or gender discrimination.

Against:

1. It's unfair to judge people by how they look. People should be selected, not judged.
2. Some experts argue that it's illegal to consider factors like age, race, gender, religion, nationality, sexual orientation, or disability status in hiring decisions.
3. Every job applicant or employee has dignity and deserves respect. It's an individual's right not to provide a photo on a resume, and that individual's right should be protected.

Task: Write down your answers here.

1) _____

_____

Unit 1 Writing a Resume

2) _____
_____

Activity 4 Distinguishing Resume from CV

Scan the QR code to watch a MOOC video about the differences between a resume and a CV. Then complete the task that follows.

Resume vs. CV

"Resume" is borrowed from a French word for "summary". In contrast, "Curriculum Vitae" (CV) is Latin for "course of life". As is suggested in its name, a CV is an overview of the accomplishments in your life. Therefore, the length of the document is variable, depending on how many experiences you have. In contrast, a resume presents a whole picture of your qualifications for a specific position, so it is generally one-page or two-pages long.

Another difference is that a CV is often used to apply for positions in academia, such as teaching or doing research in universities. So, it emphasizes academic accomplishments, including publications, patents, and presentations. In contrast, a resume is generally used to apply for positions in companies, non-profit organizations, and public sectors. So, it emphasizes professional competences and skills.

In many European countries, a CV may refer to all job application documents, including a resume. However, in the United States and Canada, the CV and resume are sometimes used interchangeably.

Task: Summarize the main points of the above passage.

Resume	CV
Length: _____	Length: _____
Purpose: _____	Purpose: _____
Emphasis: _____	Emphasis: _____
The Word Meaning in Europe: _____	The Word Meaning in North America: _____

Activity 5 Getting to Know Resume Headings

A resume is composed of a number of headings. Read a sample resume and complete the task that follows.

Jane xxx

(1) _____: Janexxx@gmail.com   (2) _____: 44 (0)20 7555666

(3) _____: 123 Park Avenue, London

(4) _____

Architect major with 2+ years of intern experience in a medium-sized company. Assisted in providing best-fit architectural solutions for two projects. Being professional, creative and innovative. Skilled in communicating with all levels of management and clients.

(5) _____

12/2019–12/2021 Intern Architect at Thinkbig Architects

- Developed and executed online, social media and print marketing strategies for the new projects.
- Participated in all phases of the design and construction processes on two international projects.
- Created 3D models and video animations.

(6) _____

08/2019–08/2022 MSc Space Syntax: Architecture and Cities at School of Architecture (UCL)

- Spatial Dynamics and Computation
- Architectural Phenomena

Unit 1 Writing a Resume

- Buildings, Organizations and Networks
- Design as a Knowledge-based Process

(7) _____

10/2020 UCL Architecture School Excellence Award Winner

12/2021 Thinkbig Architects The Year's Best Intern Award Winner

(8) _____

Public speaking, written & oral communication, teamwork, creativity, problem-solving

(9) _____

3D modeling software, video animation software, Microsoft Office, film photography

(10) _____

Singing in a choir

Playing baseball in an amateur team

Synchronized swimming

(11) _____

Available on request.

Task: Fill in the blanks with appropriate resume headings given in the box below.

| Interests | Achievements | References | Education | Address | Soft Skills |
| Phone | Technical Skills | Summary | Email | Work Experience | |

Activity 6 Making an Outline

You need to make an outline before writing a resume.

Task 1: Make an outline for your resume. You can choose the headings from the box below or create your own headings.

Resume Outline

Work Experience	Skills	Personal Details
Education	Contact Information	Objective
Interests and Hobbies	Referees	Achievements
Accolades	Awards	Certificates
Projects	Volunteering Experience	Profile/Summary

Task 2: Show your outline to your partner and answer the following questions in pairs.

1) What are the necessary headings in a resume?

2) What other headings did you include in your resume?

3) How did you decide on the priorities of those headings? (i.e. Why did one heading go before the others?)

4) How is an undergraduate's resume different from that of a person with work experience?

Unit 1 Writing a Resume

Activity 7 Comparing Resume Types

Scan the QR code to watch a MOOC video about the following three resume types and summarize their differences.

Type One: A Reverse Chronological Resume Template

Writing a reverse chronological resume means to list the latest work experience first.

Job hoppers with plenty of work experience are more likely to use this traditional type of resume. Virtually, most job applicants choose to use it.

William ×××
Street address, City, Phone, Email address, etc.
Summary …
Experience August 2017–May 2019   Company 3   Location 3
Title for Position 1
● Job responsibility 1 and achievements
● Job responsibility 2 and achievements
March 2015–August 2017   Company 2   Location 2
Title for Position 2
● Job responsibility 3 and achievements
● Job responsibility 4 and achievements
October 2012–March 2015   Company 1   Location 1
Title for Position 3
● Job responsibility 5 and achievements
● Job responsibility 6 and achievements
Education PhD in Major name
2010–2012, School name, University name
Master in Major name
2007–2009, School name, University name
Skills Proficiency in Software A, Proficiency in Language A
Interests Sports name, Recreation name, Hobby name, etc.
References Available on request.

Type Two: A Functional Resume Template

Writing a functional resume means to focus more on professional skills

Kelvin ×××
Street address, City, Phone, Email address, etc.
Objective …
Skills Summary
　　Hard Skills
　　● Skill 1 and achievements

11

relevant to the position.

This type of resume can be very helpful to recent graduates and the job applicants who want to change their job.

- Skill 2 and achievements
- Skill 3 and achievements

Soft Skills
- Skill 4 and descriptions
- Skill 5 and descriptions
- Skill 6 and descriptions

Certificates
- Certificate 1 (Time of getting it)
- Certificate 2 (Time of getting it)
- Certificate 3 (Time of getting it)

Awards and Accolades
- Award 1 (Time of getting it)
- Award 2 (Time of getting it)
- Award 3 (Time of getting it)

Education	Bachelor of Science/Arts in Major name at School name, University name
Experience	Job title at Company name, Time, Job responsibility
Interests	Sports name, Recreation name, Hobby name, etc.
References	Available on request.

Type Three: A Combination/Hybrid Resume Template

Writing a combination or hybrid resume means to mix the reverse chronological resume and the functional resume together. It places equal emphasis on both work experience and professional skills.

Diana XXX

Street address, City, Phone, Email address, etc.

Profile   …

Skills Summary
- Skill 1 and descriptions
- Skill 2 and descriptions
- Skill 3 and descriptions
- Skill 4 and descriptions
- Skill 5 and descriptions

Experience

August 2017–May 2019   Company Three   Location 3
Title for Position 1
- Job responsibility 1 and achievements
- Job responsibility 2 and achievements

March 2015–August 2017   Company Two   Location 2
Title for Position 2
- Job responsibility 3 and achievements

Unit 1 Writing a Resume

Usually, senior-level candidates with multiple experiences and versatile skills may choose to use it.	• Job responsibility 4 and achievements October 2012–March 2015 Company One Location 1 Title for Position 3 • Job responsibility 5 and achievements • Job responsibility 6 and achievements
Education	PhD in Major name 2010–2012, School name, University name Master in Major name 2007–2009, School name, University name
Interests	Sports name, Recreation name, Hobby name, etc.
References	Available on request.

Task: Fill in the table below with proper information according to the above resume templates.

Types Differences	Reverse Chronological	Functional	Combination/Hybrid
Main focus	Work experience		
Location of experience		At the bottom	
Location of skills			At the top
Possible users			

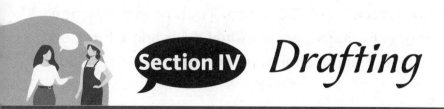

Section IV *Drafting*

Activity 8 Distinguishing Objectives from Profiles

Read a definition from the Internet about the differences between a resume objective and a resume profile/summary. Then complete the task that follows.

While a resume **objective** is a quick statement of intention for employers to know exactly what you're looking for, a **profile** of **summary** is a more holistic overview of the skills and experiences that make you the best candidate for the job.

Task: Answer the following questions.

1) What are the major differences between a resume objective and a resume profile/summary?
   _____

2) Which one of them is more suitable for a college graduate? And why?
   _____

3) Is the following sample a resume objective or a resume profile/summary?
   _____

> Motivated and ambitious recent graduate from the University of Electronic Science and Technology of China. Well-educated and systematic, have owned internship experience in China FAW Group Corporation and been trained to do a project of automatic cruising car. Seeking the work position of Integration Engineer Sensor with the passion to apply my solid knowledge to this role.

Activity 9 Creating Experience, Skills and Education History

Scan the QR code to watch a MOOC video. Then read a passage about how to list work experience, professional skills and education background in a resume. Finally, comment on the resume sections provided.

The Work Experience, Skills and Education are the crucial sections of a resume because they provide substantial information on the necessary qualifications that a job applicant desires to communicate to the potential employer. In this article, we'll show you how to compose these three sections to impress your prospective employer.

The Work Experience Section

This section is arguably the most important one in a resume. Remember this is where you start to sell yourself. After reading each description, your prospective employer wants to know where you worked, what your responsibilities were, what you have achieved, and what strengths you have. So, make your descriptions clear and concise, yet informative.

- Begin each description with the job title (e.g., intern, executive, manager), organization name, period employed and location.

- Avoid using "I", "me", "my" and any other pronouns to start a description.

- Make statements about your previous responsibilities and accomplishments with action words in past verb tense (e.g., created, supervised).

- Start with the most recent or your current job and arrange the rest in a reverse chronological order.

- If possible, add key achievements by mentioning numbers, amounts, values, and percentages (e.g., increased the sales by 20 percent).

The Skills Section

A well-written Skills section can have a positive effect on a resume because the more desirable the technical skills and qualities you have, the more attractive you will be to HR managers. Here are some tips on how to handle this section of your resume.

- Review the job description carefully and reflect upon what skills you have are on the employer's wish-list. Choose wisely.

- Include a mix of relevant hard skills (e.g., specific job skills that you learned in school or training courses, including software, foreign languages, machine operation) and soft skills (e.g., social skills or interpersonal skills, such as communication, leadership, time management).

- Back up your skills with your achievements in the Work Experience section.

- For technical skills, describe them with your proficiency level (e.g., intermediate, advanced, expert).

- Use descriptive words (e.g., adjectives and nouns) to write about the skills.

The Education Section

As one of the key sections, this part will inform employers of your background, which can be a helpful way for the employer to select candidates for the position. Although a well-experienced HR manager can scan your education section with a glance, there still exists something valuable that can stand you out.

- Follow a reverse chronological order.
- Start with the name of your degree (e.g., B.A., MBA., PhD) and your major, connecting them with the preposition "in".
- Give the name of your school, college, or university, followed by period attended and location.
- Include your minor or second major as well.
- Optionally list some academic achievements (e.g., GPA, honors, scholarship), and courses or exchange programs that are relevant to the position.

Now that you've got all about how to write the crucial parts of a resume, try to work on your own. We believe you can succeed.

Task: Comment on the resume sections below.

Work Experience

Online Marketing Assistant

Linemart, Amsterdam, 04/2018–08/2020

- Created online franchise website for the company
- Helped gathering sales data with computer marketing tools
- Ran a survey using Google Surveys to discover users' satisfaction with the products

Online Marketing Manager

Linemart, Amsterdam, 09/2020–present

- Increased revenue
- Launched 3 advertising campaigns in overseas markets

---

1) _____

_____

_____

_____

Unit 1 Writing a Resume

Skills
- Technical Skills
  C++, Python
  Advanced in English (CET 6), Intermediate in Japanese
  Problem-solving
- Soft Skills
  Graphic design
  Effective communication
  Critical thinking

2) _____

Education
University of California, Berkeley
2016-2012
B.Sc. in Electronic Information Engineering
GPA 3.8

3) _____

Activity 10 Using Proper Language

The language of resume has its own features. Appropriate expressions can give your resume a plus.

Task: Find out the error types of the following sentences from the options in the box and improve them to make them appropriate for a resume.

1) I always love integrated circuits and I hope to make my own useful products (as is written for Objective).

2) Design an algorithm which can enhance the reliability of information in the communication of inserted-system (as is written for Work Experience).

3) Responsible for e-commerce data mining, analyzing the trend of keywords, market capacity and competition (as is written for Work Experience).

4) B.A. of English Language and Culture (as is written for Education).

5) As a head of a student association for a year and volunteer teaching in a remote area twice (as is written for Work Experience).

6) Have good abilities of stress management and self control (as is written in Skills).

> A. Having "I", "me", "my" in the statement
> B. Using a verb in a noun phrase
> C. Lacking a verb in the statement
> D. Lacking an action word
> E. Using the wrong verb tense
> F. Using a wrong preposition

1) Error type (　　)

_____

2) Error type (　　)

_____

3) Error type (　　)

_____

4) Error type (　　)

_____

5) Error type (　　)

_____

6) Error type (　　)

_____

Unit 1 | Writing a Resume

Activity 11 Understanding the Unit Project

Write your own resume to apply for a vacancy in Tesla China. You should start by studying the job advertisement below and getting to know its job responsibilities and requirements. If you have work experience, you should base the resume on your work experience; if you are a college undergraduate, you can write about what you will do in job hunting.

Role:

IT Manufacturing Support Technician

- Job category: Engineering & Information Technology
- Location: Shanghai
- Req. ID: 78460
- Job type: Full-time

Tesla has an opportunity for an IT Manufacturing Support Technician at Shanghai Lin Gang. If you are a technical expert in various areas, thrive under pressure, enjoy solving problems, love working your way through chaos, and get bored with mundane IT tasks, then this role is for you. The IT Manufacturing Support Technician is a unique role on the front of lines of Tesla manufacturing. We solve problems every day and interact with different technologies to support Tesla's mission to accelerate the world's transition to sustainable energy.

Job Responsibilities:

- Primary responsibility is to keep manufacturing lines running.

- Install, support, upgrade, replace, and troubleshoot all IT hardware issues along manufacturing lines.
- Quickly respond to requests and incidents from our customers.

Job Requirements:

- Must have good communication skills.
- Linux support experience a plus.
- Network hardware support experience a plus.

(Retrieved from Tesla China website.)

Task: *Write down your answers here.*

_____
_____
_____
_____

Section V Reflection

Activity 12 Choosing a Layout

When it comes to resume layout, some industries like legal service, banking, finance, etc. require a more traditional style in the layout (as shown in Picture 1), while sectors like technology, advertisement and innovation value creativity in layout style (as shown in Picture 2).

Picture 1　Traditional Style

RESUME

Personal Information

Name　　　Zhang
Address　　2006 Xiyuan Avenue Chengdu Sichuan
Tele　　　　xxx
Email　　　zhang@xxx.com
WeChat　　xxx

Objective

Creative recent graduate with a B.E. majoring in opto-electronics from the University of Electronic Science and Technology of China. 6 months of work experience in Tencent. Looking to grow as an engineer to solve tricky problems at Google.

Experience

Class Committee
Organized class dinners and cooperated the college in organizing events like competitions between classes.

Internship at Tencent
Worked at Tencent for 6 months and helped the company create a skin for a mobile game hero.

Education

The University of Electronic Science and Technology of Chengdu, Sichuan, China July 2019
Undergraduate degree in Opto-electronics Information Science and Engineering
GPA: 3.91/4.0
Key course: Physical Optics, Applied Optics, Digital Signal Processing

Skills

Technical Skills　　C++, Matlab
Language　　　　　English
Certifications　　　CET 4, CET 6
Interests　　　　　　Basketball

References

Li
Professor, School of Foreign Languages, UESTC
li@xxx.com

Liu
Professor, School of Opto-electronics, UESTC
liu@xxx.com

Picture 2　Creative Style

Personal Resume

 OBJECTIVE

- An awareness of public relations, excellent communication skills, event planning and coordination skills.
- Good attitude and sense of responsibility, hard-working, good at management, brave to face challenges.
- Looking to constantly improve myself as a Recruitment Coordinator and make my own contribution to the development of the company.

 EDUCATION

University of Electronic Science and Technology of China

B.E. in Information Engineering　　　　　　2019.9–2023.6

- GPA 3.8/4.0　　　　Rank:17/122

 EXPERIENCE & PRACTICE

Assistant Network Culture Construction Office　2019.10–Now

Main responsibility：Construction of network culture

- Assisting to hold the National Internet Summit　　　2020
- Assisting to hold national network culture exhibition activities　2021

President Student Union of the College of Opto-electronic Science and Engineering　　　　　　　　2020.5–Now

Main responsibility：Organize various intercollegiate activities

- Organizing a basketball game for students of the college　2020
- Organizing a party with the College of Opto-electronic of Sichuan University　　　　　　　　　　　　　　　2020
- Organizing voluntary activities with the Logistics Department of the university　　　　　　　　　　　　　　　2021

 AWARDS

second-class scholarship of the university　　　2020
National Computer Rank Examination Level 2　　2021
M class of the Interdisciplinary Contest in Modeling　2021

Mason

📍 University of Electronic Science and Technology of China

📱 xxx

✉ Mason@xxx.com

🏠 Chengdu, Sichuan, China

SKILLS

Hard

CET6

Word

Excel

Powerpoint

Ps

Cantonese

Mandarin

Soft

Leadership

Creativity

Applicant Position

The Recruitment Coordinator

Unit **1** Writing a Resume

Task: Reflect upon your resume for Tesla China in Activity 11. What is the layout for your resume? And is it suitable for the organization and position you are applying for?

My resume style is _____ because _____
_____
_____

Activity 13 Tailoring Your Resume

Read the following sample resume for Tesla China's IT Manufacturing Support Technician and complete the task that follows.

RESUME

Name: X X X

Tel: +86 X X X   **Email:** X X X @uestc.com   **Address:** X X X

Objective

Passionate recent graduate with a B.E. in Computer Science from University of Electronic Science and Technology of China seeking new opportunities. Two years of practical experience studying in Artificial Intelligence and Deep Learning in an eminent professor's laboratory. Looking forward to grow as an Advanced Driver Assistance Systems (ADAS) Engineering Technician with sustainable developing opportunities.

Work Experience & Achievements

Member in State Key Laboratory of Artificial Intelligence and Deep Learning

8/2022–4/2023, UESTC

- Dedicated in prompting relative algorithm and published an article in a SCI journal.
- Won the Innovation & Uniqueness in Design Award for the outcome.

Intern in Huawei (Shenzhen) Company

8/2022–9/2022, Huawei(Shenzhen)

- Learned fundamental coding skills and got considerable salary.
- Acted as an assistant of algorithm designer and got internship certificate.

Team Member of College Students Volunteer Association

10/2019–10/2022, UESTC

- Took part in Village Supporting Education Planning and got the certificate.
- Left a deep impression on kids in the village and got praised by the leader.

Leader of an Entrepreneurship of College Students Group

10/2020–10/2021, UESTC

- Put forward a creative and practical idea and got highly supported by college.
- Led the team and won the First Award of Sichuan Competition Area.

Vice President of Science and Innovation Association

08/2019–06/2020, UESTC

- Organized the official website on GitHub and won Excellent Member Prize.
- Schemed the "Taking in the Fresh" plan and got high praise.

Education

B.E. in Computer Science

University of Electronic Science and Technology of China

08/2019 – 06/2023

Award

UESTC Computer Science Department Excellent Student Award Winner

Key Courses

- Data Structure and Algorithm
- Computer Compose Principle
- Computer Network
- Computer Operator System

Skills

Technical Skills

- Coding in Python to create Web Crawlers and conduct Deep Learning
- Using C/C++ to design and mend a brand-new algorithm frame
- Having the Front-end Development ability to finish HTML documents independently
- Taking advantage of GUI to provide users with a personalized visual interface

Unit 1 Writing a Resume

- Having the capability of creating independent video projects with Adobe Premier Pro

Soft Skills

- Acting as a group leader to organize a series of activities required
- Skilled in resolving the conflicts in diverse situations
- Being able to create innovative ideas with critical and far-sighted thinking

Interests

- Playing basketball, badminton and table tennis
- Reading books of Nietzsche
- Listening to classical and pop music
- Being exposed to a brand-new technology area

References

Available on request.

Task: Do you think the resume above has tailored the information to the descriptions of the job advertisement in Activity 11? Make some comments by giving evidence from the resume.

My major opinion is:

_____

_____

My evidence includes:

_____

_____

_____

_____

Activity 14 Doing a Peer Review

Scan the QR code to watch a MOOC video about resume writing skills. Then ask your partner whether your resume is reader-friendly or not. Then do a peer review with your partner by using the following checklist.

Questions	Answers	
Is your partner's resume one-page or two-pages long?	Yes ☐	No ☐
Are your partner's fonts easy to read?	Yes ☐	No ☐
Does your partner pick different font sizes for the headings?	Yes ☐	No ☐
Does your partner have enough white space and margins?	Yes ☐	No ☐
Does your partner use multiple bullet points?	Yes ☐	No ☐
Does your partner use a table for the resume?	Yes ☐	No ☐

Section VI Exposition

Activity 15 Revising Your Resume

Revise your resume based on both of your self-reflection and the reader's feedback. Print out your revised version and submit it to your teacher.

Activity 16 Assessing the Unit Product

Organize a resume exposition in which groups of students score a number of submitted resumes in Activity 15 and finally select 5 best-written ones. Use the following scoring table for help.

Number	Names	Total	Dimensions	Scores	Weights	Specifications
1			Language		40%	**Language** refers to accuracy in spelling, punctuation, grammar and appropriateness of word choice. **Content** concerns the resume type, the heading use, the clarity, conciseness and the informative quality of the resume. **Effects** mean to what degree the resume information and layout style are tailored to the job advertisement, and whether the resume is reader-friendly as a whole.
			Content		40%	
			Effects		20%	
2			Language		40%	
			Content		40%	
			Effects		20%	
3			Language		40%	
			Content		40%	
			Effects		20%	
4			Language		40%	
			Content		40%	
			Effects		20%	
5			Language		40%	
			Content		40%	
			Effects		20%	

Section VII Wrap-Up

Activity 17 Conducting Self-Evaluation

Use the following scale to self-evaluate your knowledge about writing a resume and how well you have done in learning this unit. Four in the right column means you totally agree with each statement on the left, while zero means you totally disagree with it.

Statements	Degree of Agreement
I can distinguish a resume from a CV.	0 1 2 3 4
I can decide what headings are necessary for my resume.	0 1 2 3 4

(Continued)

Statements	Degree of Agreement
I can choose an appropriate type of resume according to my career stage.	0 1 2 3 4
I can choose an appropriate layout style that is in line with the organization's sector characteristics.	0 1 2 3 4
I can tailor my resume information to meet the requirement of a job advertisement.	0 1 2 3 4
I can write my resume in a professional way.	0 1 2 3 4
I can create a reader-friendly resume.	0 1 2 3 4
I have already had my resume proofread.	0 1 2 3 4
I have become less anxious to write another resume.	0 1 2 3 4
I have enlarged my vocabulary related to resume writing.	0 1 2 3 4

Unit 2
Handling a Job Interview

商务职场沟通英语

  Section I *Warm-Up*

Activity 1 Initiating the Unit

People tend to be nervous in a job interview because answering questions from the employers makes them feel vulnerable or exposed. Research shows recalling famous quotes can help people to calm nerves and overcome fear.

Task: Read the following quotes and think about which one(s) can encourage you to face a job interview bravely. Tell your partner the one(s) you choose and why.

1) Choose a job you love, and you will never have to work a day in your life. —*Confucius*

2) You never know how strong you are until being strong is your only choice. —*Bob Marley*

3) Start by doing what is necessary, then what is possible, and suddenly you are doing the impossible. —*Francis of Assisi*

4) One important key to success is self-confidence. An important key to self-confidence is preparation. —*Arthur Ashe*

5) Success is not final, failure is not fatal: It is the courage to continue that counts. —*Winston Churchill*

Activity 2 Understanding the Key Concept

Phil Smith is answering a phone call from Arcmark Technology. Read the conversation in pairs and complete the task that follows.

Emily: Good morning, may I speak to Phil Smith?

Phil: Yes, speaking.

Unit 2 Handling a Job Interview

Emily: Mr. Smith, this is Emily from the HR of Arcmark Technology. We've received your email saying you want to join us.

Phil: Oh, yes. I'm very interested in your vacancy for a sales manager.

Emily: Very good! I've read your resume. It's very impressive. Now, I'd like to invite you to come over for an interview.

Phil: Sure, I can do that. When do you need me to be there?

Emily: If you can come next Monday at 10 a.m., I'll make an appointment for you to meet our **interview panel**.

Phil: No problem. Next Monday morning at 10 o'clock.

Emily: Great! See you then.

Phil: Bye.

Task: Explain what an interview panel is in your own words.

_____

_____

You can check the reference here.

Knowledge Notes

The interview panel is a group of interviewers from different departments within a company. The interviewers ask questions about the job vacancy and they work together to decide whether to hire the candidate or not. The interview that involves candidates and an interview panel is called a panel interview.

Section II Pre-speaking

Activity 3 Describing Qualities

 Scan the QR code to watch a MOOC video about what key qualities employers admire.

Task: Find more qualities that you think important for a job seeker. Hold a group discussion to explain why you choose them. Some words and phrases are offered in the box below. You can choose to use them when you speak.

The qualities I admire are _____

because _____

ability to learn	communication	creativity	ability to socialize
professionalism	accountability	loyalty	stress management
leadership	diligence	ambition	self-discipline

Activity 4 Analyzing What Quality Matters

 Scan the QR code to watch a movie clip from *The Pursuit of Happiness* and complete the task that follows.

Task: Answer the following questions related to the movie clip.

1) What happened to Chris the day before the interview?
2) What did Chris wear for his interview?
3) What qualities did Chris think the interviewers may admire?
4) What questions did the interviewers ask about Chris' qualifications?
5) Were Chris' answers satisfactory?

Unit 2 Handling a Job Interview

6) What did Chris finally say to save himself?
7) What key qualities won Chris the job?

Activity 5 Finding out the Admirable Qualities

What key qualities are the employers in China looking for? Go to ask some other people who have more work experience than you.

Task: Ask your family, friends and other acquaintances: What three key qualities does your employer or organization expect from the employees? Collect your answers by using the table below and share them with your class.

Who You Asked	What the Qualities Are	Why They Matter
1) _____ 2) _____ 3) _____ …	1) _____ 2) _____ 3) _____ …	1) _____ 2) _____ 3) _____ …

Section III *Planning*

Activity 6 Dressing for Success

Scan the QR code to watch a MOOC video about how to dress for a job interview. Then read the following passage and complete the task that follows.

Dressing for Job Interviews

On a formal occasion, men should wear a suit and tie, and women should wear professional attire. While in a casual setting, you can wear a jacket, a shirt and smart trousers. No matter what you wear, keep the color conservative and solid. Remember that clothing for an interview should be appropriate. So, for women, don't show too much flesh when wearing a skirt. Never be overdressed. Too many jewelry or accessories can be a distraction for other people. Avoid wearing a hat because it may make you look like getting something to hide. Pay attention to your personal hygiene. Take a shower before you go to the interview; and for men, don't forget a shave. Perfume may not be allowed to use in some interviews. Last but not the least, whatever you wear, make sure your clothes fit properly and you will be comfortable in it.

Task: **Look at the four people below and decide which candidate's dressing is the most appropriate for a job interview. Share your reasons with your partner by using the words in the box below.**

| flesh | hat | conservative | professional | overdressed |

Activity 7 Mastering Non-verbal Skills

Scan the QR code to watch a MOOC video about some key non-verbal skills. Then read the following passage and complete the task that follows.

The Key Non-verbal Skills for Job Interviews

How you dress yourself, how fast you speak, what hand gestures you make, whether you use eye contact, etc., are all so-called non-verbal behaviors. Candidates' non-verbal behavior may probably decide the interviewer's impression about them. In her book *The Non-verbal Advantage*, Carol Kinsey Goman stresses that one only gets seven seconds to leave a lasting first impression. So, if you want to grab the interviewer's attention in such a short time, the following five tips will help you make it.

(1) Stand tall. Stand up straight, pull your shoulders back, and hold your head high. This physical position will make you feel sure of yourself.

(2) Smile. A smile expresses two meanings. The first is an invitation, a sign of welcome. It says you are friendly and approachable. The second is a label of confidence. It says you are ready.

(3) Make eye contact. Looking at someone's eyes transmits positive energy, conveys honesty and determination, and indicates interest and openness.

(4) Lean in slightly. Leaning forward when sitting shows you are engaged and interested. In the perspective of psychology, we naturally lean towards people we think we like or agree with.

(5) Shake hands firmly. Make sure to hold the other person's hand a few seconds longer than you're inclined to. This conveys additional sincerity.

Seven seconds may be short for making a positive first impression, but if you handle it well, seven seconds are all you need.

Task: Look at the three pairs of pictures and decide which one in each pair shows the most appropriate non-verbal behavior. Share your reasons with your partner by using the words in the box below.

1)

Picture A

Picture B

| firm | second | sincerity |

2)

Picture A

Picture B

| straight | shoulder | head | confident |

3)

Picture A

Picture B

| lean | engage | agree | slouch |

Unit 2 Handling a Job Interview

Section IV Practicing

Activity 8 Identifying the Question Types

Scan the QR code to watch a MOOC video about various types of job interview questions. Then read a passage about the same topic and complete the task that follows.

Various Types of Job Interview Questions

If you're preparing for a job interview, it's really important for you to make a plan, including considering various types of questions you might be asked. The first one is the **background question**. Questions of this type are the most common in an interview. They are education-related, work-experience-related, or private-life-related. The candidates are expected to confirm their credentials when answering a background question. An **opinion question** looks for a candidate's subjective viewpoint or attitude towards a problem, issue, or situation. By asking it, the interviewers gain a chance to assess the candidate's critical thinking and decision making skills. **Behavioral questions** focus on a candidate's behaviors at past workplaces or in school settings. The theory behind it is that someone's past behavior is the best indicator of his future behavior. Therefore, this type of question is often put into a context or scenario to stimulate answers. That's why behavioral questions are also called situational questions. The last type is the **puzzle question**. As it often tests the candidate's logic and maths skills, it is also called the brainteaser. Some brainteasers don't seek for a single right answer because they are designed to evaluate the candidate's creativity or the ability to analyze information.

Task: Identify the types of the following questions.

1) Which course did you find the most difficult during your college?

2) How would you improve your GPA if you had a chance to re-do the course?

3) How tall is a piece of paper folded 25 times?

4) Do you think the world is really flat now?

Activity 9 Answering Background Questions

Scan the QR code to watch a MOOC video about how to answer three background questions. Then read a passage about the same topic and complete the task that follows.

The interview might be kicked off with the question: "Tell me about you." This open-ended question could be the trickiest one because the candidates are not expected to spend much time talking about their whole life story. On the contrary, the candidates should give an insight into what experiences, skills and qualifications they have are most relevant to the position they are interviewing for.

The recipe for this question contains three steps, involving the past, present and future respectively:

- Tell your major successes at work or greatest achievements at school. (the past)
- Mention your current job responsibilities or most recent work experience. (the present)
- Focus on your key skills and strengths that will help you do the job well. (the future)

You are usually expected to give an answer within two minutes, with examples if necessary. Here is a sample from a postgraduate candidate:

I've been passionate about industrial designing since I entered my university. During my postgraduate study, majoring in Automation Engineering, I was on a research team working on a project to develop a monitor of the next generation that can acquire and display oscilloscope waveform with higher sensitivity.

My previous experience of doing research and development has built up my proficiencies in signal modulation and waveform collection. The most rewarding part of my experience is I'm able to apply cutting-edge theoretical approaches and technologies to the clients' practical demands.

Moving forward, I'd love to take an active part in the company's project of waveform collection. I believe that my knowledge and skills will eventually help your company. And my experience and passion will allow me to be a great asset to your research and development team.

The next question asks "Why should we hire you?" or "Why should the company offer you the job?" There are two major reasons why the interviewers ask this question.

First of all, they need to know your uniqueness that can separate you from the other candidates. And then, they need to know whether you have done your research and understand the job well. Accordingly, in order to answer this question effectively, you need to follow the steps below:

- Show you know the job description and understand the roles very well.
- Tell your uniqueness and explain how it fits the position.
- Be confident and show your motivation and enthusiasm about the job.

An example is provided for you:

As I can see from your job descriptions, you want a new project manager who is capable of handling the affairs with new international clients as a result of your fast-growing overseas business.

Frankly speaking, I think I'm just the man for this role! I'm a brilliant planner and good communicator who is a proficient speaker of English, Spanish and Italian. I've taken over two underperforming sales teams and managed to achieve their KPIs within only three months. I've doubled our customer numbers in South America.

With all my expertise and previous achievements, I'm confident that I would fit perfectly in this position you are offering.

The last question is "What is your biggest weakness?" By asking you the question, the interviewers want to know your self-awareness and your willingness to improve. Therefore, it isn't wise to shun or dodge the question. It is also unwise or even absurd to confess a genuine deficiency or defect. So, what are expected to be said in the response is as follows:

- Pick something less important or just a flaw in doing the job.
- Show your initiative with some methods to improve yourself or what you have already done to overcome it.
- If possible, turn a negative into a positive.

Let's learn an example from an undergraduate:

In response to this question, I think my biggest weakness is that I may become a little nervous when I am doing a presentation or giving a public speech. Specifically, it depends on how large the audience is. It won't always happen, especially when there is a small number of audience. Normally, I can deliver my representation in high quality and handle the Q&A session actively. Now, I'm following an online English course to enhance my public speaking skills.

Task: Based on what you have learned from the above passage, can you select which of the following answers best responds to each of the questions below? Share your reasons with the class.

1) Can you tell me about yourself?

> As a biotech major, I can help the company to deal with most of the thorny problems that I have been trained to address. And I am a good learner and willing to master the knowledge that I am interested in.

2) Why should the company offer you the job?

> If your company is looking for an unparalleled planner to lead the sales team, I think I am just the right person. With my brilliant marketing strategies, my previous employer has established key footholds in Europe last year. Actually, I've got some ideas to help your company to improve the profits. I love challenges and I have confidence in this role.

3) What is your biggest weakness?

> I think my biggest weakness is my introverted disposition. I am quiet and a little shy. I know doctor-patient relationship is extremely important. Doctors are supposed to communicate with patients and their family very often, like calming the patients' nerves. However, it's pretty hard for me. Maybe I'll get used to it after becoming a doctor.

Activity 10 Answering Behavioral Questions

Scan the QR code to watch a MOOC video about the formula for answering behavioral questions. Then read a passage about the same topic and complete the task that follows.

The Formula for Answering Behavioral Questions

A proven effective formula to answer behavioral questions (or situational questions) is known as the **STAR** formula. It breaks into three steps: one, describing the **situation** or **task**; two, speaking about the **action** you took; and three, offering the final measurable **result**.

The formula is illustrated in the following picture.

Unit 2 Handling a Job Interview

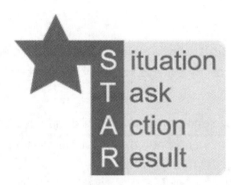

As for applying the formula to answer questions, you can follow the steps below:

S: Detail the situation. Provide the context, such as who, where and when.

T: Describe the expectation and challenge. What is needed to be done? Why?

A: Elaborate a specific action. What did you do? How? What methods and tools did you use?

R: Explain the results, accomplishments, recognitions, etc. Quantify them if possible.

Task: According to the STAR formula, which of the following two answers is well-structured? Share your reasons with the class.

Question:

   Could you give an example of a difficult situation that you've faced? How did you solve it? What was the outcome?

Answer 1:

   The most difficult situation I've ever encountered was when I was invited to join in a scientific research project. As a sophomore, I had no experience of doing any projects. It was undoubtedly very challenging for me. After thinking it over for hours, I was in.

   In my team, some teammates and I were responsible for doing experiments and writing the final paper. At the beginning, we searched tons of relevant studies in the library and on the Internet to decide the goal of the project. After that, I came to the mentor's lab to carry out a series of experiments, followed by data recording and analyzing. The most difficult part was that when starting to write the paper, I conquered a large number of research papers in English by using a translation software.

   With such great efforts, I accomplished my first project paper within two weeks. To my surprise, my project ended with excellence and won the second prize.

Answer 2:

> One of my difficult situations was when I joined in an electronic design contest in the second semester of my college. I can still remember how I worked with the other two students.
>
> When we started, we encountered a lot of difficulties because we didn't have skills or experience. There were many things we needed to learn. Frustrated as we felt, none of us gave up.
>
> After two months' preparation and hard work, we finally made it through and won the third prize. After the contest, I suddenly realized what perseverance means and why it matters.

I think Answer _____ is well-structured because _____

Activity 11 Giving It a Try

Siemens China offers on-campus vacancies to excellent Chinese college graduates. Suppose you were asked the following question during an on-campus interview this year:

Maybe you've had a situation where you had a very difficult team to work in. Can you give me an example and just describe the situation?

Task: Read the following job advertisement of Siemens China to understand its job responsibilities and requirements. Prepare your own answer to the above question and share it with your partner.

Unit 2 Handling a Job Interview

Role:

Head of Digital Manufacturing Technology

Job Responsibilities:

- Responsible for PCBA manufacturing process for industry automation product, including SMT (surface-mount technology), THT (through-hole technology), AOI, SPI, in-line lasering, in-line automation, etc., ensure PCBA manufacturing process and product quality.

- Collaboration with R&D team / factory teams to create and optimize responsible process, and continuous improvement.

- Data analytics with SW coding and development or IT tool.

Job Requirements:

- Bachelor and above

- Electric information engineering, Software engineering, Automation engineering, Statistics, Computer, etc.

- Capable of IT, and data analytics

- Advanced English in both oral and writing

(Retrieved from Siemens website.)

  **Section V** *Reflection*

Activity 12 Reinforcing the STAR Formula

Scan the QR code to watch a video about a sample answer to the Siemens China's interview question in Activity 11. Then complete the task that follows.

Task: Review the STAR formula in Activity 10 and analyze the structure of the sample answer in the video by following Questions 1–3 below. Next, reflect upon Questions 4–6 and discuss them in class.

1) What difficult situation was the interviewee in?
   _____

2) What did the interviewee do to make the situation more friendly?
   _____

3) What was the final result?
   _____

4) Why was the interviewee interrupted when answering the question?
   _____

5) Did the interviewee use the STAR formula to organize his ideas? If not, what was wrong with the first part of the answer?
   _____

6) How should we improve the answer with the STAR formula?
   _____

Activity 13 Improving the Answers

Read the transcript of the video in Activity 12 and complete the task below.

Task: Interview answers must be succinct and persuasive. Think about how to make the following answers more succinct and persuasive with the help of the drawback analyses below.

Drawback 1: Containing information irrelevant to the question.

The interviewer:	Maybe you've had a situation where you had a <u>very difficult team to work in</u>. Can you give me an example and just describe the situation?
The interviewee:	Okay. Well, I think I had that situation before, but not in this IT company. It was when I was doing the music program for a radio

Unit 2 Handling a Job Interview

> company. And that was really a bad experience because <u>the place I worked in</u> was very small, like a room with only five or six square meters and with other equipment, CDs and tapes. And there was only <u>one-person place</u> left for me to do my program and I had to go there four times a month, once a week. And that's actually not the worst thing.

1) My improvement is: _____
   _____
   _____
   _____

Drawback 2: Containing unnecessarily repetitive and redundant information.

> **The interviewee:** And that's actually not <u>the worst thing</u>. <u>The worst thing</u> is that <u>the people there</u>, including <u>my employer and my so-called "teammates"</u>. They just <u>don't take me as a member</u>. They <u>don't think I'm a member of them</u> or not even a staff there.

2) My improvement is: _____
   _____
   _____
   _____

Drawback 3: Mentioning ineffective problem-solving skills.

> **The interviewer:** Did you try to do something with the team members to make the situation or environment a little more friendly?
>
> **The interviewee:** I did. I tried to <u>hang out with them</u> and <u>talk to my employer and my teammates</u>, but it just didn't seem to work. As my employer said, she probably just wanted a money relationship, just that pay-you-the-money-you-do-the-job relationship.

3) My improvement is: _____
   _____
   _____
   _____

Drawback 4: Expressing a negative outcome in the end.

The interviewee: That's what…that's not what I expected. So, finally, after half a year I decided to quit.

4) My improvement is: _____

_____

_____

_____

Activity 14 Doing a Peer Review

Improve your answer to the Siemens China's interview question in Activity 11 by using the techniques you have just learned in Activity 13. Then do a peer review with your partner by using the following checklist.

Questions	Answers
Does your partner's answer describe the situation or task clearly?	Yes ☐ No ☐
Does your partner's answer offer specific actions to deal with the above situation?	Yes ☐ No ☐
Does your partner's answer end with a measurable result?	Yes ☐ No ☐
Is your partner's answer succinct?	Yes ☐ No ☐
Does your partner's answer have unnecessary repetition or redundancy?	Yes ☐ No ☐
Does your partner's answer use effective problem-solving skills?	Yes ☐ No ☐
Is the result of your partner's answer positive?	Yes ☐ No ☐

Section VI Exposition

Activity 15 Understanding and Assessing the Unit Project

Organize a mock job interview in class. Some students play the interviewer's role while others act as interviewees. Each interview panel (having two or more students) is responsible for offering vacancy information (containing job roles, responsibilities and requirements), preparing interview questions (including background questions, opinion questions, behavioral questions and brainteasers), and scoring for the interviewees' performance. All the vacancy information and the interview questions need to be offered to the interviewees before the interview. After the interview, the interviewers should select the best candidates. Use the following scoring table for help.

Number	Name	Total	Dimension	Score	Weight	Specifications
1			Language		30%	**Language** refers to accuracy in spelling, pronunciation, grammar and appropriateness of word choice. **Content** concerns the quality of the answers, including what elements and structure they should have; how detailed and vivid they are; to what degree the answers are tailored to the post; and whether they are relevant, succinct, persuasive and satisfactory. **Delivery** means how skillful the verbal and non-verbal techniques can be intentionally used to achieve the purposes.
1			Content		40%	
1			Delivery		30%	
2			Language		30%	
2			Content		40%	
2			Delivery		30%	
3			Language		30%	
3			Content		40%	
3			Delivery		30%	
4			Language		30%	
4			Content		40%	
4			Delivery		30%	
5			Language		30%	
5			Content		40%	
5			Delivery		30%	

Section VII Wrap-Up

Activity 16 Conducting Self-Evaluation

Use the following scale to self-evaluate your knowledge about dealing with a job interview and how well you have done in learning this unit. Four in the right column means you totally agree with each statement on the left, while zero means you totally disagree with it.

Statements	Degree of Agreement
I can identify the key qualities I have to get the job.	0 1 2 3 4
I can dress myself appropriately for a job interview.	0 1 2 3 4
I can answer background questions appropriately in a job interview.	0 1 2 3 4
I can answer behavioral questions appropriately in a job interview.	0 1 2 3 4
I can use non-verbal skills appropriately in a job interview.	0 1 2 3 4
I can use the STAR formula to answer questions.	0 1 2 3 4
I can tailor my answers to the intentions of different questions.	0 1 2 3 4
I can provide succinct answers to the interview panel.	0 1 2 3 4
I can provide persuasive answers to the interview panel.	0 1 2 3 4
I have become less anxious to handle another interview.	0 1 2 3 4
I have enlarged my vocabulary related to job interviews.	0 1 2 3 4

Module II

Making Business Connections

Unit 3

Writing an Email

商务职场沟通英语

Section I Warm-Up

Activity 1 Initiating the Unit

Emails have long been widely used for both business and private affairs. Recall and share your own experiences of using emails.

Task: Choose a topic from the following two options and share your own experience or idea with a partner. Some phrases are offered in the box below. You can choose to use them when you speak.

1) If you often send or receive emails, talk about the purpose for which you usually write emails.

2) If you seldom use emails, talk about why you prefer other means of communication, e.g., QQ or WeChat, to emails.

chat with friends	send a job application	receive important notices
share pictures and videos	receive junk emails	check the inbox
reply to an email	on the mobile phone	

Activity 2 Understanding the Key Concept

Linda and Jack are talking about how to use emails during their internship. Read the conversation in pairs and complete the task that follows.

Lina: Hi, Jack. How about your internship?

Jack: It's OK, I believe. Not a lot of real work to do, but it's really a big challenge for me to handle so many emails every day.

Lina: Emails? That may take lots of time.

Unit 3 Writing an Email

Jack: Yeah, I didn't realize people send so many emails. You know, before this, I hardly use emails. We've got QQ and WeChat, and they are much more convenient.

Lina: You are right. But now you are not just a college student. You work for a big company.

Jack: True. There are a lot of things I need to learn, like sending and receiving **attachments**.

Lina: How hard can that be?

Jack: I mean, you need to use certain expressions to ask others to check the attachment, or respond to their attachments. That's something quite new to me.

Lina: I see. That sure is not so easy.

Task: Explain what an email attachment is in your own words.

_____

_____

You can check the reference here.

> **Knowledge Notes**
>
> An email attachment is an additional computer file that is sent along with the email message. It is a quite simple and convenient way to share some images or documents with the email receiver.

Section II Pre-writing

Activity 3 Distinguishing Two Types of Emails

Read a passage about the differences between personal and corporate-based emails and complete the task that follows.

Differences Between Personal and Corporate-Based Emails

Security Features

You can be relatively sure that your email use isn't being monitored in your personal email. The corporate email, on the other hand, should be considered an open book to your employer, since it is maintained and paid for by a company that wants the accounts to be used for business purposes.

Etiquette

Though you might send a casual email to a family member or a funny picture to a friend from a personal email account, the same should not be done from a corporate-based email account. Corporate email messages should be checked carefully for grammatical or spelling errors; they should include your full name and the full name of the recipient; they should not include any abbreviations or Internet language.

Cost of Accounts

The cost of personal and corporate emails also varies greatly. Many people get free personal email accounts from Internet service providers. When a business wants to offer employees a corporate-based email account, it usually incurs a significant cost. However, if corporations can offer free email accounts for employees, these accounts will come with a corporate domain and will look more professional.

Task: Answer the following two questions related to the above passage.

1) Why does a corporate email cost more than a personal email?

   _____

   _____

2) Is it still worthwhile for a company to pay for corporate email service? Why?

   _____

   _____

Activity 4 Distinguishing Business Letters from Business Emails

Read a passage about business letters and business emails and complete the task that follows.

Business Letters and Business Emails

Business letters follow more or less a formal style and reserved voice while business emails typically take the informal route and use a less strict style.

Business letters, while in transit, maintain the confidentiality of their content better than business emails. Why? It's because the email message travels to its destination via the Internet—the public network. With advancements in email security technology like secure protocols and encryption, however, the potential for the wrong eyes to read a business email is much lower.

If you need the proof of receipt of your communication, the business letter route serves you the best. It is true that many desktop email clients today have the return receipts feature. However, whether the email client will deliver an acknowledgement depends on whether your customer uses one of such email software and whether he/she has enabled the feature.

When the phrase "global warming" has become a house-hold name, it's widely acceptable to use business emails, as much as possible, to save the earth. The lesser the business letters you use for communication, the lower the number of trees that will go under the axe. Make your business greener with emails, e-documents, and digital information.

Task: Put a tick in the right box for the features that business letters or business emails have. An example has been given.

Features	Business Letters	Business Emails
Formal and reserved	√	
Informal and less strict		
Better confidentiality		
Reliable acknowledgement		
Environment-friendly		

Section III Planning

Activity 5 Mastering Email Essentials

Read the following email sample and complete the task that follows.

Task: Fill in the blanks with the words in the box below.

(1) _____ :	bethcollins@nashpr.com
(2) _____ :	russjackson@gmail.com
(3) _____ :	(information omitted here)
(4) _____ :	(information omitted here)
(5) _____ :	New Book
(6) _____ :	📎 Press Release.doc

Unit 3 Writing an Email

(7) _____,

I thought you might be interested in our new book, *How to Write a Business Email*, which can benefit your readers.

Please let me know if you would like to see a copy or would be interested in speaking with the author. In the attachment there is the text of our press release.

I look forward to hearing from you.

(8) _____,

Beth Collins

(9) _____

Nash Public Relations

360 Madison Avenue, Suite 103

(10) _____

212-602-4008

Subject	Attachment	From	Dear Mr. Jackson
Bcc	New York, NY 10011	Director of Publicity	Cc
Best regards	To		

Activity 6 Mastering Email Structure

Read a passage about the main structure of a business email and complete the task that follows.

The Three-Section Structure

After the salutation (Dear… / Hi…) and before the sign-off (Best wishes / Yours sincerely), an email is usually composed of three sections: introduction, body and closing.

The introduction/opening section includes your opening sentence which has your name or states the intent of the message. Add additional sentences if necessary, but keep it brief and don't exceed three sentences.

The length of the body section might vary depending on the industry, but don't exceed three paragraphs (or 15 sentences in total). Use this section to further explain your interests and give more details that you consider necessary.

The closing section acts as your final thoughts and call-to-action. It is usually an invitation for your reader to take some action: join a meeting, sign up for a service, or just simply check your attachment. By using friendly, polite and professional language with a clear call-to-action, you have a better chance of earning a positive response.

Task: Study the following example email whose opening, body and closing are not clearly marked out. You need to go through the long paragraph and divide it into three parts with the double slash "//".

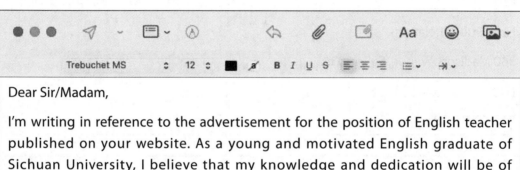

Dear Sir/Madam,

I'm writing in reference to the advertisement for the position of English teacher published on your website. As a young and motivated English graduate of Sichuan University, I believe that my knowledge and dedication will be of value to your college and your students. I've been involved in various activities of the university, which has allowed me to develop strong interpersonal and organizational skills. In addition, I have learned the value of rewards of hard work and dedication throughout my academic life and I'd like to join your school in striving for excellence. Therefore, I'd consider myself an ideal candidate for this position.

My resume is attached for your consideration. If I can provide you with any further information on my background and qualifications, please let me know.

Thank you very much for your time.

Yours sincerely,

Anna Smite

Unit **3** Writing an Email

Activity 7 Identifying Email Sections and Purposes

Read the four email examples below and complete the tasks that follow.

Task 1: Decide which paragraph (A or B) in the following box is the opening and body of each email.

Example 1:

Dear shareholders,

Opening: _____

Body: _____

Please let us know if you can attend by clicking this link CLICK HERE by February 15, as we need a quorum to hold the meeting as scheduled.

Thank you for your time, and we hope to see you on May 12.

Kind regards,

Jessica Murphy

A

We have attached a meeting agenda to this email so you know what to expect. The meeting will cover the following key topics:

- Elections to fill this year's board openings
- Votes on shareholder proposals
- Annual financial reports
- New developments

B

As the time for our annual general meeting approaches, we'd like to thank you for your ongoing support. We hope you will attend this year's meeting, which we have scheduled for May 12, 2022, at 10 a.m. on Zoom. You'll find the link here. CLICK HERE

59

Example 2:

Dear Mr. Tate,

Opening: _____

Body: _____

I apologize for any inconvenience you may have experienced and hope that you'll continue to do business with us in the future.

Thank you,

Anthony Romano

A

Thank you for contacting us about the damaged product you received. I am very sorry this has happened and wish to make it right for you.

B

I am sending a replacement product, which I personally inspected for damage before shipping.

Example 3:

Dear Mrs. Scott,

Opening: _____

Body: _____

I would really appreciate it if you could deal with these matters urgently.

I look forward to hearing from you.

Yours sincerely,

Carter Freeman

Unit 3   Writing an Email

A

First of all, could you please provide us with an update on where you are on the Airport Project? We would also appreciate it if you could clarify what the current issues with the delivery system are, and confirm when you expect them to be resolved.

In addition, at the end of our last meeting we requested a copy of the latest project update report. Unfortunately, we have still not received it. We would appreciate it if you could forward this to us.

B

I am writing in reference to the current situation with the Airport Project. We have a number of questions which we hope you could answer.

Example 4:

Dear Mr. Thomson,

Opening: _____

Body: _____

In case you are interested to know anything about our firm, feel free to contact us at the address and contact details on the brochure.

Thank you for your time.

Sincerely,

Sarah Black

A

The purpose of this email is to introduce Investin to you, a firm that has been active in the investment business for the last two decades. We are proud to inform you that we have some of the biggest clients spread all across Europe and the US, and we have been successful in providing them with efficient services.

61

B

Along with this email, we have attached brochures, documents, and information pamphlets about our firm. After going through these information sources, you will be able to know that we are working in diversified investment fields, such as mutual funds, equity shares, life insurance, etc. We offer our services after thorough counseling with our clients and by charging a nominal fee.

Task 2: Go through the above four opening parts again, and find which sentences in each part present the purposes given in the following table. Write these sentences down in the corresponding blanks. An example has been given.

Purposes	Examples	Expressions Used
Gratitude & invitation	1	1) *We'd like to thank you for your ongoing support.* 2) _____
Gratitude & apology	2	1) _____ 2) _____
Demand	3	1) _____
Introduction	4	1) _____ 2) _____

  **Section IV** *Drafting*

Activity 8 Being Concise and Direct

Read the following two sample emails and complete the tasks that follow.

Task 1: Discuss in pairs which one is better written and give your reasons.

Unit 3 Writing an Email

Example 1:

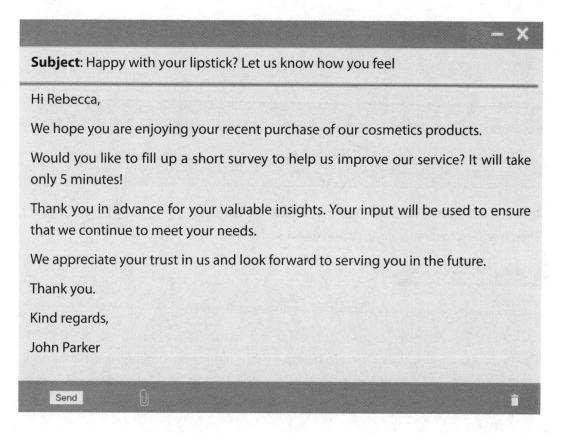

Subject: Happy with your lipstick? Let us know how you feel

Hi Rebecca,

We hope you are enjoying your recent purchase of our cosmetics products.

Would you like to fill up a short survey to help us improve our service? It will take only 5 minutes!

Thank you in advance for your valuable insights. Your input will be used to ensure that we continue to meet your needs.

We appreciate your trust in us and look forward to serving you in the future.

Thank you.

Kind regards,

John Parker

Example 2:

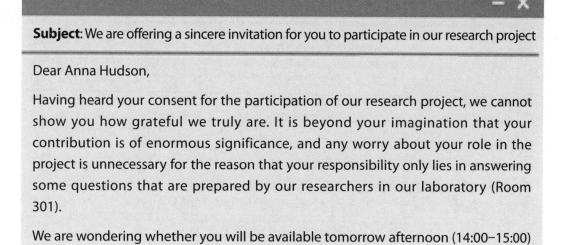

Subject: We are offering a sincere invitation for you to participate in our research project

Dear Anna Hudson,

Having heard your consent for the participation of our research project, we cannot show you how grateful we truly are. It is beyond your imagination that your contribution is of enormous significance, and any worry about your role in the project is unnecessary for the reason that your responsibility only lies in answering some questions that are prepared by our researchers in our laboratory (Room 301).

We are wondering whether you will be available tomorrow afternoon (14:00–15:00) when we do not have plans for other interviewees.

We are looking forward to your reply.

Best wishes,

Lily Dawson

Send

I think _____ is better because _____

_____

Task 2: Read the Knowledge Notes below and find the language problems in Example 2. Then rewrite it in a more concise and direct style.

Knowledge Notes

Make It Concise and Direct

Most people have zero patience for overly long emails or those that don't immediately convey the complete picture. Therefore, it is essential to be direct and concise when writing business emails. Keep the sentences brief and concise, and avoid complex structures and unnecessary big words.

Subject:

Hi Anna,

Send

Unit 3 Writing an Email

Activity 9 Using Call-to-Actions

Read the Knowledge Notes below and complete the task that follows.

> **Knowledge Notes**
>
> ### What Is a Call-to-Action?
>
> A call-to-action is a brief statement that asks readers or consumers to respond with a specific action or participate in something. It can be a phrase, text, or a button asking them to make a purchase, make a phone call, read your blog post, and so on.

Task: Work in pairs and choose the most suitable call-to-action from the box below to make the following email complete and coherent. Talk about why the other two choices are not appropriate.

Dear Sir or Madame,

I hereby write to introduce my company which I started a year ago. Packers is a packaging company that manufactures refillable bottles that can be reused. We have recently entered the US market and I wish to inform you of the products we manufacture.

…

_____ I wish to arrange a meeting so that we can discuss our partnership.

I look forward to your response.

Best regards,

Oliver Anderson

A. Don't you think it is a good idea to partner with us?
B. I would like to propose that you partner with us.
C. It is a good opportunity for you to partner with us.

Activity 10 Improving the Language

Read the sentences below and complete the task that follows.

Task:

Find out the error types of the following sentences from the options in the box and improve them to make them appropriate for emails.

1) The reason I write this email is we have some problems with the latest shipment of products from your plant.

2) Our company recently purchased your printers and we have been very disappointing since the beginning of use.

3) We should like to make this right by sending you another sweatshirt in the color that you have ordered.

4) I apologized for any inconvenience you may have experienced and hoped that you would continue to do business with us in the future.

5) Could you send me more information about the meeting schedule.

6) Thank you for purchasing our online course, and I hope our online course serves you well.

7) We are looking forward to see you at the meeting next Monday.

A. Using a wrong preposition
B. Repeating the same words
C. Using a wrong modal verb
D. Using the wrong form of a verb
E. Using a wrong punctuation
F. Using a wrong clause
G. Using the wrong verb tense

---

1) Error type (   )

_____

2) Error type (   )

_____

Unit 3 Writing an Email

3) Error type (   )

🧰 _____

4) Error type (   )

🧰 _____

5) Error type (   )

🧰 _____

6) Error type (   )

🧰 _____

7) Error type (   )

🧰 _____

Activity 11 Understanding the Unit Project

Read a brochure about a trade fair event and write an email to invite George Anderson, the marketing manager of a sporting goods manufacturer, to join the event. Suppose you are the marketing director of Shanghai International Trade Fair, and you have met him once three months ago at an industry conference.

The Shanghai International Trade Fair

Purpose

The Shanghai International Trade Fair has been widely known for many years as an effective showcase for Pacific Rim products. It is first and foremost a trade fair to stimulate new Asian market opportunities and develop those already established for Pacific Rim imports exclusively.

Duration and Place

Shanghai New International Expo Centre (SNIEC) houses the trade fair from April 23 to April 29 this year. There are exclusive buyers' hours during the day. At night, the Fair as a large public show, attracts thousands of visitors from Shanghai and all parts of East Asia.

Sponsors

The Fair is a non-profit enterprise sponsored by the Shanghai municipal government, the Port of Shanghai, prominent business, industrial, commercial and transportation firms, labor, civic and cultural organizations.

Merchandise

Quality workmanship and originality are quickly recognized and accepted by store buyers, wholesalers and importers. Among most popular items are products of native craftsmanship, home furnishings, fabrics, sporting goods, camera and optical equipment.

Buyers

Ten thousand retail store buyers, importers, wholesalers and distributors from all over China, the US, Japan and other countries have been invited. Buyers will come to make personal contact with you, buy your goods, arrange for future buying or become your representatives.

Task: Write an email based on the information in the above brochure. You should use your own words and not directly copy from the brochure. You should write about 100 words.

Unit 3 Writing an Email

 Section V *Reflection*

Activity 12 Analyzing a Sample

Read a sample email for Activity 11 and complete the task that follows.

Subject: Trade Fair Invitation

Dear Mr. Anderson,

I hope everything has gone well since we met in Los Angeles three months ago. I'm writing to invite you to participate in our trade fair, which will take place at SNIEC.

The trade fair has great influence around the Pacific Rim, and many firms from different countries will attend the event. Sporting goods are also one of the most

商务职场沟通英语

> important kinds of merchandise. Thus it's a great opportunity for your company to meet all the buyers.
>
> Just let me know if you have any questions about the event.
>
> We sincerely look forward to your reply.
>
> Best regards,
>
> Tom Wang

Task: Do you think the above email has summarized all the key information in the brochure in Activity 11? In fact, at least two pieces of information are missing. Can you point out what information should be added to the sample?

The missing information includes: _____

_____

_____

_____

_____

Activity 13 Paying Attention to Your Tone

Below are three different opening sentences that state the purpose of the email assigned in Activity 11. Read the sentences and complete the tasks that follow.

1) I think you must be interested in our trade fair this year, and the details are as follows.

2) I'm sorry if this email disturbs you, but I hope maybe you will give me a few minutes to introduce our trade fair, so that probably you will consider attending this event.

3) It's my pleasure to invite you to our trade fair, which will take place at Shanghai New International Expo Centre (SNIEC) from April 23 this year for 7 days.

Unit 3 Writing an Email

Task 1: Work in pairs and discuss which of the above sentences is the most appropriate and why the other two are not.

The most appropriate opening sentence is _____ because _____
_____

The problems with the other two sentences are as follows:
_____
_____

Task 2: Read a passage about the tone of an email and review the email you wrote in Activity 11 to see if you used the appropriate tone.

The Tone of an Email

In emails, tone is the attitude you want to present to the recipient. Your email tone can convey many attitudes, such as professionalism, friendliness or optimism. Choosing the appropriate tone for your email ensures that the message you send is easy for the reader to interpret, which helps you start or maintain a strong relationship.

The tone of an email reveals the writer's emotional state towards the reader or the subject. When you write emails, you can use many different tones to convey your meaning and help the reader understand your message. Learning how to use the right tone in your emails will ensure that you build and maintain professional relationships with coworkers, managers and clients.

Activity 14 Doing a Peer Review

Ask your partner to give you some feedback on your email for Activity 11. Then do a peer review with your partner by using the following checklist.

Questions	Answers
Is there a clear and concise subject?	Yes ☐ No ☐
Has your partner used warm and friendly greetings?	Yes ☐ No ☐
Is there a follow-up for the previous encounter with the recipient?	Yes ☐ No ☐
Has your partner put forward his/her purpose at the beginning of the email?	Yes ☐ No ☐

(Continued)

Questions	Answers	
Is all the important information included?	Yes ☐	No ☐
Is there a clear call-to-action in the closing part?	Yes ☐	No ☐
Is there a signature?	Yes ☐	No ☐
Is there an accurate use of punctuation?	Yes ☐	No ☐
Has your partner used proper capitalization?	Yes ☐	No ☐
Are the sentences concise and easy to read?	Yes ☐	No ☐
Has your partner used easy-to-understand vocabulary?	Yes ☐	No ☐
Has your partner avoided the problem of repetition?	Yes ☐	No ☐
Is there a consistent tone throughout the email?	Yes ☐	No ☐
Has the email already been proofread?	Yes ☐	No ☐

Section VI *Exposition*

Activity 15 Revising and Submitting Your Email

Revise your email based on your self-reflection and your partner's feedback. Print out your revised email and submit it to your teacher.

Activity 16 Assessing the Unit Project

Organize an email exposition where groups of students score a number of submitted emails in Activity 15 and select 5 best-written ones. Use the following scoring table for help.

Number	Name	Total	Dimension	Score	Weight	Specifications
1			Language		20%	**Language** refers to accuracy in language use and appropriateness of word choice. **Content** concerns the email structure, the clarity and conciseness of the email. **Effects** mean to what degree the email has fulfilled the function as an invitation, and whether the email is reader-friendly as a whole.
1			Content		40%	
1			Effects		40%	
2			Language		20%	
2			Content		40%	
2			Effects		40%	
3			Language		20%	
3			Content		40%	
3			Effects		40%	
4			Language		20%	
4			Content		40%	
4			Effects		40%	
5			Language		20%	
5			Content		40%	
5			Effects		40%	

Section VII Wrap-Up

Activity 17 Doing Self-Evaluation

Use the following scale to self-evaluate your knowledge about writing business emails and how well you have done in learning this unit. Four in the right column means you totally agree with each statement on the left, while zero means you totally disagree with it.

Statements	Degree of Agreement
I know all the essentials of a business email.	0 1 2 3 4
I can distinguish business emails from private emails.	0 1 2 3 4
I can understand the concept of email attachments.	0 1 2 3 4
I can set the tone for my email.	0 1 2 3 4
I can write about a subject concisely and efficiently in my email.	0 1 2 3 4
I can choose to use different greetings based on different recipients.	0 1 2 3 4
I have written a satisfactory first draft in Activity 11.	0 1 2 3 4
I find my partner's feedback on my email writing helpful.	0 1 2 3 4
I can reply to a business email.	0 1 2 3 4
I have improved my writing skills in this unit.	0 1 2 3 4

Unit 4

Receiving Visitors

商务职场沟通英语

 Section I *Warm-Up*

Activity 1 Initiating the Unit

What are your favorite jobs? And which one is your dream job? Imagine the job you will do in the future.

Task 1: Design a desk sign for your dream job and include the information listed in the bubble below.

Your name,
Your job title,
Your company

Task 2: Work in groups and simulate attending social events. You will keep talking with different group members until you have completed the following steps.

Step 1 Greeting each other;

Step 2 Introducing yourself;

Step 3 Explaining why you come to the event;

Step 4 Meeting two more people and repeating Steps 1, 2 and 3.

Activity 2 Understanding the Key Concept

Mike is a sales manager and Mai is a newly-recruited intern working under Mike. One day they are talking about how to break the ice with strangers in communication. Read the conversation in pairs and complete the task that follows.

Mike: Good morning, Mai. How is everything going?

Unit 4 Receiving Visitors

Mai: Good morning, Mike. It's pretty good. How are you?

Mike: I'm good, too. Yesterday, HR Department asked me to do a training session for the new employees. I'm just thinking about a suitable topic. Do you have any suggestions?

Mai: I always feel it's a little bit hard to break the ice with strangers in communication, especially in business situations.

Mike: Yes, it's not easy. When I was a newbie at work, I always wondered how to start and what topics I should bring forward. I was afraid I would have said something wrong to offend people.

Mai: Me too!

Mike: **Small talk** is a good choice to break the ice in communication. It is a light and informal conversation. Making small talk may not be stress-free, but if you go into it with an open mind, you may actually have some fun.

Mai: What topics are appropriate for small talk?

Mike: Ah, a lot of topics can work, such as job, weather, travel, holiday, sports, etc. For each topic, asking some engaging questions may encourage conversations and get interesting information.

Mai: Sounds fun. How about sharing your experience of small talk with us?

Mike: Good idea! Let me think about it. Thank you.

Mai: You are welcome. I'm looking forward to it.

Task: Explain what small talk is in your own words.

_____

_____

You can check the reference here.

Knowledge Notes

In most English-speaking countries, it is normal and necessary to make "small talk" in certain situations. Small talk is a casual form of conversation that "breaks the ice" or an awkward silence between people. Even though you may feel shy using your second language, it is sometimes considered rude to say nothing. Just as there are certain times when small talk is appropriate, there are also certain topics that people often discuss during these moments.

商务职场沟通英语

Section II Pre-speaking

Activity 3 Distinguishing Two Ways of Communication

Read a passage about two different ways of communication and complete the task that follows.

Face-to-Face Communication vs. Telephone Conversation

  The main difference between face-to-face communication and telephone conversation is that the former is more personal than the latter. You can see the person's facial expressions and gestures and how he/she reacts.

  Face-to-face communication is a way of social interaction which allows the person to communicate with another person directly. It can be physical, with one person seeing another person's behavior, facial expressions, gestures, etc. But telephone conversation is cheaper and consumes less time than meeting the person face-to-face as it would be more expensive to visit someone in another city.

  When it comes to geographical locations and shortage of time, face-to-face communication may not be the best option. Therefore, phone calls, emails, etc., are preferred. Telephone conversation is the most important form of communication in the modern era. Without it, a lot of work may be pending. By using the telephone, you can talk with someone in a couple of minutes.

Task: Complete the following table that summarizes the above passage for the differences between face-to-face communication and telephone conversation. You need to decide on the comparison aspects first. An example has been given.

Aspects of Comparison	Face-to-Face Communication	Telephone Conversation
Time and cost	It requires arrangement of time and it is usually costlier.	It is efficient and usually doesn't cost much.

Activity 4 Understanding the Unit Project

Read the rubric of the unit project below. Then hold a quick discussion with other group members to make sure you fully understand the project. You can choose your own favorite companies and change the background information provided. However, you cannot change the task objectives your group should achieve in this activity.

Background Information: Joy Sports, a profitable Chinese sportswear manufacturer, buys its products from suppliers all over the world. The Marketing Department of Joy Sports is establishing business connections with FIT, a multinational sportswear retailer based in London. To achieve its goal, Joy Sports is going to receive a visit from FIT's vice-president Joseph Patrick. As a sales executive in Marketing Department, your task objectives include:

Objective 1: Call FIT to confirm the time and date of the network video conference to finalize the details of Patrick's approaching visit;

Objective 2: Make a one-day schedule to entertain Patrick during his visit;

Objective 3: Meet Patrick and other FIT's staff at the airport;

Objective 4: Have a formal Chinese dinner with Patrick and the FIT delegation.

Don't start your project until you proceed to Activity 15 where you will read more requirements. Before you can tackle the above tasks, you should learn more skills through the following series of activities.

Section III *Planning*

Activity 5 Choosing Suitable Topics

Read a passage about the suitable topics for small talk and complete the task that follows.

Best Small Talk Topics

Small talk topics are good conversation starters between people who don't know each other well. Sometimes, making small talk can be anxiety-provoking. It can also be difficult if you are more introverted. Learning to make small talk can help build the confidence you need to start conversations, make connections, and develop your social skills. Even if small talk makes you uncomfortable, avoiding it will only exacerbate anxiety in the long run. Rather than being scared of small talk, try to overcome your fear of it. A good way to alleviate anxiety is to know what things to talk about and what to avoid.

If you are looking for some good conversation starters, here are a few topics to consider.

Good Topics	Bad Topics
Weather	Finances
Arts and entertainment	Politics and religion
Sports	Sex
Family	Death
Food	Appearance
Work	Personal gossip
Travel	Offensive jokes
Celebrity gossip	Narrow topics
Hobbies	Past relationships
Hometown	Health

Weather

Although talking about the weather may seem mundane, it is a good neutral topic that everyone can discuss. Did a big storm just blow through? Are you in the middle of a heatwave?

Look no further than outside your door for conversation starters such as:

- Lovely day, don't you think?
- Looks like rain is in the forecast.
- Did you order this beautiful weather?

Practice making small talk about the weather by asking someone one of these questions the next time you find yourself in the middle of an awkward silence. They may open up other topics as the conversation progresses.

Arts and Entertainment

Arts and entertainment topics that are good conversation starters include: movies, television shows, popular restaurants, popular music and books.

Examples of things you might ask are:

- Are you reading any great books? I could use some recommendations.
- Are there any podcasts you love?
- Have you tried any new apps or games lately that you really like? I could use some suggestions.

Skip talking about movies, television, or books that your conversation partner has not seen or read. If no one else has seen the movie, don't go into detail about the plot or the funny scenes. Find some common ground and build your discussion from there.

You might have to ask several people before you get someone interested in talking with you—that's okay. Be okay with rejection, or actually seek it out. It's all just practice, after all.

Sports

Sports topics are good things to talk about with people you don't know very well. They can include: favorite or local teams, sporting events, tournaments or championships.

Keep track of what sports are played during which seasons—such as football, soccer, hockey, and golf—so you are on top of the current action. The Olympic Games are always a good option if they are taking place, as everyone is sure to be buzzing about them.

If your conversation partner supports a rival team, avoid trash-talking. Instead, focus on keeping your discussion on things like team or player performance.

Ask someone, "Did you catch that golf tournament over the weekend?" While this might feel uncomfortable the first few times you do it, eventually, it will feel more natural to you.

Family

People are likely to ask you about your family. Conversation starters about family may include:

- Do you have any brothers or sisters?
- How long have you been with your partner?
- Where does your family live?

Be prepared for these types of questions and reciprocate by asking others about their families. Engaging in this type of small talk displays your communication skills. It also helps you learn a lot about a person in a short period of time.

Although family can be a great conversation starter, use it cautiously when asking about potentially sensitive topics. For example, asking someone if he/she has kids or plans to have kids can be difficult if that person is experiencing infertility. If the other person has children, however, feel free to ask about them.

Food

Food can be a great topic for small talk as long as you keep it neutral and focus on the positive. You might ask someone for recommendations for local restaurants, ask what their favorite dish to order is, or if he/she enjoys cooking at home.

Some examples of food-based topics include:

- Have you tried any new restaurants lately?
- What's your favorite meal to cook at home?
- Do you have any ideas for good work lunches? I'm out of ideas and I'm sick of sandwiches.

As with other conversation starters, stick to positive topics and avoid complaining about foods you dislike.

Unit 4 Receiving Visitors

Task: Study a conversation that illustrates small talk and answer the following questions.

Yao and Iryna are coworkers, bumping into each other in the coffee room of the company.

Yao: Hi, I am Yao from the Accounting Department.

Iryna: Nice to meet you, Yao. I am Iryna from the Sales Department.

Yao: I have never met you before. Are you new here?

Iryna: Yes, it is my first work day.

Yao: Wow, congratulations. How is everything going?

Iryna: It's quite good. Actually, I have been transferred from the headquarters.

Yao: I see. Have you got used to the weather here? Recently, it's raining all the time, very humid.

Iryna: I am fine. It's also very humid in London now. But according to the weather forecast, this weekend will be sunny and breezy.

Yao: That must be very comfortable. What do you usually do at the weekends?

Iryna: I often bike with my family and friends at the weekends. Bicycling provides me with another way of looking at the city and the people.

Yao: I totally agree with you. I enjoy bicycling too. Maybe we could bike together in this city to see what you may find.

Iryna: That would be fantastic. I couldn't wait to explore this new city by bike.

1) What topics have been covered in the conversation?
   _____
   _____

2) Are there any other suitable topics for small talk at work? Give some examples.
   _____
   _____

Activity 6 Paying Attention to Phone Expressions

Study a phone conversation and complete the task that follows.

Receptionist: Ivy Consulting. What can I do for you?

David: Hello, I want to talk to Ms. Ann, the general manager of your company.

Receptionist: Who is speaking, please?

David: I'm David from Sunny Agency. There is an urgent issue I need to discuss with her.

Receptionist: Excuse me, do you have an appointment?

David: Sorry, I don't. But it's really urgent. Could you check with her right now?

Receptionist: Hold up. I will get back to you immediately.

…

Receptionist: Thanks for waiting. Ms. Ann is available and I'm transferring your call.

David: Thank you very much.

Receptionist: Sure.

Task: Some everyday expressions are not suitable to be used in phone conversations. Can you work with a partner to recognize the inappropriate expressions in the above phone conversation and replace them with appropriate ones?

Activity 7 Making a Schedule

Read a passage about how to make a sightseeing schedule for company's guests and complete the task that follows.

Making a Schedule for Your Guests

It is important to make a schedule so as to use time effectively. What should be considered when making a schedule to entertain your business guests? First of all, the available time for both hosts and guests should be checked. Then, do some research on the guests' sightseeing preferences, since some people would like to experience a bit local life and some may prefer to visit a famous place of interest. If time is limited, the priorities in the schedule should be jotted down, and given more time. Besides, the transportation and traffic to the places should also be considered, especially in cities where traffic jam at rush hours is a routine. Tasting local food is also something that a lot of people would enjoy. Pick a suitable restaurant with local flavor for your guests, but be aware of the different eating habits among people.

Task: If your business guests are free in the afternoon and evening, what will you take into consideration while making a schedule to entertain them? Have a group discussion to fill in the planning table below and then report your schedule to the class.

Suggested Activities	Time Allocation	Considerations

Activity 8 Mastering Chinese Business Etiquette

Scan the QR code to watch a video about Chinese business etiquette. Then complete the task that follows.

Task: Write down the dos and don'ts of Chinese table manners in the following table. Besides, add some more rules at the end of the table.

Aspects	Dos	Don'ts
Dressing	*The suit is in a conservative color.*	*Wear too short skirt for women.*
Giving a business card		*Give the card with one hand.*
Exchanging gifts		
Having a dinner		
Drinking white liquor		
Additional rules		

Section IV *Practicing*

Activity 9 Practicing Phone Conversations

Suppose you are a sales executive in the Marketing Department of Joy Sports introduced in Activity 4. You need to call Mr. Smith from FIT to confirm the time and date of the network video conference to finalize the details of Joseph Patrick's approaching visit (See Activity 4).

Task 1: Check out the following main steps in telephone communication and offer one or two sentences for each step.

1) Introduce yourself formally:
   _____
   _____
   _____

2) Explain the purpose of your calling:
   _____
   _____
   _____

3) Suggest the time for the network video conference:
   _____
   _____
   _____

4) Double-check the information:
   _____
   _____
   _____

Unit 4 Receiving Visitors

5) Close the call:

_____

_____

_____

Task 2: Work with a partner and take turns to be the caller and the receptionist in the following situations to make a brief telephone conversation. Some sentence patterns are provided for you in the box below.

1) The caller with appointment is calling to talk to Mr. Smith, the general manager.
2) The caller with no appointment is calling to talk to Mr. Smith, the general manager.
3) The caller is calling to talk to Ms. Green, but she is not in the office.
4) The caller is calling to talk to the PR manager but has dialed the wrong number.

I would like to talk to…	May I speak to…
May I know who is calling please?	Hold a second.
I will transfer your call to…	I am afraid…
Would you like to leave a message for…?	May I take a message for…?

Activity 10 Making an Entertaining Plan

Before Mr. Patrick and FIT delegation's departure, a schedule should be made and sent to them.

Task: Make a one-day schedule to entertain Mr. Patrick from FIT (introduced in Activity 4). You can also refer to the list you have come up with in Activity 7.

A One-Day Schedule

Time	Suggested Activities	Highlights	Transportations
Morning			
Afternoon			
Evening			

商务职场沟通英语

Activity 11 Meeting Your Guests

Role-play the following conversation with your partner. Then complete the task that follows.

Mr. Hilton: Excuse me, are you Mr. Li from the Agricultural Support?

Mr. Li: Yes. Mr. Hilton?

Mr. Hilton: Yes, I'm Robert Hilton from the Rice Origin Foundation.

Mr. Li: I'm Qing Li. Very nice to meet you. Welcome to Shanghai!

Mr. Hilton: Thank you very much for picking me up at the airport.

Mr. Li: You are welcome. Is this your first time to China?

Mr. Hilton: This is my second time to China, but very first time to Shanghai. I'm very excited to come to this famous city of China.

Mr. Li: Shanghai is very international. I hope you will like it here and have a pleasant stay. By the way, how is the flight?

Mr. Hilton: It's OK. I've been used to long-distance flights.

Mr. Li: That's good. Our car over there is to take you to the hotel. Let me take the luggage for you.

Mr. Hilton: Thank you!

Mr. Li: You are welcome. You may have a good rest today. Tomorrow morning, I will wait for you at the hotel lobby at 9 o'clock and take you to our company.

Mr. Hilton: Sounds good.

Task: Suppose you are meeting Joseph Patrick and other FIT's staff at the airport. Work with a partner who acts as Mr. Patrick and make a conversation by covering the following steps.

Step 1 Greet and introduce yourself and your colleagues to each other;

Step 2 Ask about the experience of taking the flight;

Step 3 Ask about the first impression of the arrival city;

Step 4 Help carry the luggage and lead the guests to the car;

Step 5 Brief the arrangement for your guests on the way to the hotel.

Unit 4 Receiving Visitors

Activity 12 Analyzing Intercultural Conflicts

Scan the QR code to watch the video from the movie *The Joy Luck Club*. Then complete the task that follows.

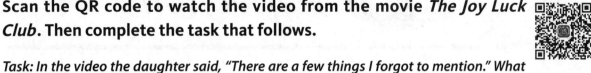

Task: In the video the daughter said, "There are a few things I forgot to mention." What are Richard's should-have-not's?

1) _____

2) _____

3) _____

4) _____

Section V Reflection

Activity 13 Reflecting on Your Phone Call Skills

Scan the QR code to watch a video about the suggestions for effective business phone calls. Use the given checklist below to reflect on your sentences in Activity 9.

Questions	Answers
Did you introduce yourself formally?	Yes ☐ No ☐
Did you explain your calling purpose clearly?	Yes ☐ No ☐
Did you use constructive words when making suggestions?	Yes ☐ No ☐
Did you do active listening when dealing with the phone conversation?	Yes ☐ No ☐
Did you cram chunks of information in what you said?	Yes ☐ No ☐
Did you double-check the information with the call receiver?	Yes ☐ No ☐
Did you show politeness in your call?	Yes ☐ No ☐
Did you reach the goal of your call?	Yes ☐ No ☐

Activity 14 Designing Your Own Checklists

Work in pairs to design your own checklists to reflect upon your performance in the following two activities. A checklist template is provided below for your reference.

1) The one-day schedule to entertain Mr. Patrick in Activity 10;
2) The conversation to meet and receive Mr. Patrick and FIT delegation at the airport in Activity 11.

A checklist template:

Questions	Answers
	Yes ☐ No ☐
	Yes ☐ No ☐
	Yes ☐ No ☐
	Yes ☐ No ☐
	Yes ☐ No ☐
	Yes ☐ No ☐
	Yes ☐ No ☐
	Yes ☐ No ☐

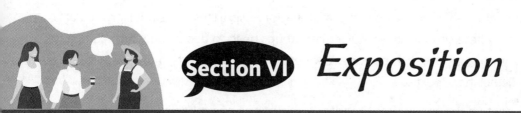

Section VI *Exposition*

Activity 15 Conducting the Unit Project

Review the rubrics of Activity 4 and then follow the rubrics of this activity below.

Task: Divide the whole class into eight groups. Four groups play as the multinational sportswear retailer FIT or other companies you have chosen, while the other four groups act as the Chinese sportswear manufacturer Joy Sports or other companies you have chosen. Then, you should complete the steps below.

Step 1　Sportswear retailers need to specify the location of the company, business range, major consumers, strengths of the brand, etc. Sportswear manufacturers need to specify the location of the company, business range, major clients, competitiveness of the company, etc. Each group is given two minutes to do their presentation. A company card is recommended to be used in this step.

Multinational Sportswear Retailers (Group _____)	
Location of the company	
Business range	
Major consumers	
Strengths of the brand	

Chinese Sportswear Manufacturers (Group _____)	
Location of the company	
Business range	
Major clients	
Competitiveness of the company	

Step 2   After the self-introduction, the multinational sportswear retailer groups and the Chinese sportswear manufacturer groups need to decide on which company they want to establish business connections with. Every two groups will work together in the next steps.

Step 3   Every two groups gather together to exchange some basic information, such as staff names, personal preferences of food, cultural taboos, etc., for three minutes. A personal information card is recommended to be used in this step.

My Personal Information (Group _____ Student Name _____)	
Staff name	
Staff position	
Staff gender	
Ethnic group	
Personal preferences	
Cultural taboos	

Step 4   Every two groups work together to complete the following four tasks, the process of which should be videotaped for further assessment.

Unit 4　Receiving Visitors

1) One executive of the Chinese sportswear manufacturer calls the multinational sportswear retailer to confirm the time and date for an online video conference that will finalize the detail of the leader's approaching visit.

2) At least two executives of the Chinese sportswear manufacturer make a one-day schedule to entertain the leader during the visit.

3) One executive of the Chinese sportswear manufacturer meets and receives the leader and the delegation of the multinational sportswear retailer at the airport.

4) At least two executives of the Chinese sportswear manufacturer have a Chinese dinner with the leader and the delegation of the multinational sportswear retailer.

Activity 16　Assessing the Unit Project

The videotapes of Activity 15 should be sent to the class for peer review and the teacher's assessment. The scoring table is provided for you below. Rate five aspects of the groups' performance marked A, B, C, D and E with numbers from 1 (poor) to 5 (excellent).

Groups	Aspect A	Aspect B	Aspect C	Aspect D	Aspect E	Total Score

Evaluation aspects:

Aspect A: Communication over the phone is appropriate and effective.

Aspect B: The one-day schedule is feasible and appealing.

Aspect C: The way of meeting and receiving guests at the airport is proper and smooth.

Aspect D: Food and table manners are suitable and comfortable for guests.

Aspect E: The overall communication is effective and appropriate.

商务职场沟通英语

Section VII Wrap-Up

Activity 17 Conducting Self-Evaluation

Use the following scale to self-evaluate your knowledge about receiving visitors and how well you have done in learning this unit. Four in the right column means you totally agree with each statement on the left, while zero means you totally disagree with it.

Statements	Degree of Agreement
I can introduce myself properly on formal occasions.	0 1 2 3 4
I understand the meaning and significance of small talk.	0 1 2 3 4
I can break the ice in communication with strangers.	0 1 2 3 4
I am aware of the language difference between talking over the phone and talking face-to-face.	0 1 2 3 4
I can make an appointment over the phone.	0 1 2 3 4
I can make a schedule for certain purpose.	0 1 2 3 4
I can pick up a foreign guest at the airport.	0 1 2 3 4
I am aware of the intercultural conflicts over the table.	0 1 2 3 4
I have enlarged my vocabulary related to business connections.	0 1 2 3 4

Unit 5

Giving a Presentation

商务职场沟通英语

 Section 1 *Warm-Up*

Activity 1 Initiating the Unit

 Scan the QR code to watch a video that introduces a company and then complete the task that follows.

Task: Answer the following questions. Some words and expressions are provided for you in the box below.

1) What do you learn about the company?
   _____
   _____

2) Who is the possible audience of the video?
   _____
   _____

3) What are the possible purposes of the video?
   _____
   _____

corporate introduction	potential customer
investor	persuade the client
distributor	advertise products or services
introduce discounted service	attract investment opportunities
social media marketing tool	business partner

Unit 5 Giving a Presentation

Activity 2 Understanding the Key Concept

Jim works for Sweet Life Snack Food Company, a snack food manufacturer based in New York, US. Jim's friend Mary is giving him some suggestions about a job assignment he received. Read the conversation in pairs and complete the task that follows.

Mary: Hi Jim, what happened? You look worried.

Jim: Oh, I'm in trouble. My boss asked me to give a presentation to some new clients next Monday. I have no idea what to do. Where should I start?

Mary: What is the presentation about?

Jim: A **corporate profile** of our company, but it is such a small snack company. What can I say about it? I'm afraid my talk won't last for five minutes.

Mary: Are you kidding? There are so many awesome things to share.

Jim: Really? What can I say? Any suggestions?

Mary: Sure. For example, who started the company?

Jim: Our president of course!

Mary: I know, but what is his name? What prompted him to get into the snack food business? What mission does the company set out to accomplish?

Jim: Wait, wait. I think I know what you mean. I can tell the story about our company. That would be interesting.

Mary: Yeah, but not just that. You can review the history and look into the future as well. For example, how has the company developed all these years? What is the future vision? Do you have a five-year or ten-year plan?

Jim: Right! It is a great chance to show them what a solid foundation we have and how much potential we possess. Wow!

Mary: Yeah. And don't forget to take this opportunity to advertise your products and promote your business...

Jim: Oh, it is so exciting. Now I've got a million fantastic ideas. I can't wait to start now! Thank you so much!

Task 1: Explain what a corporate profile is in your own words.

_____

_____

You can check the reference here.

Knowledge Notes

A corporate profile is an introduction to a company. It includes some business details such as the company's name, address, phone number and working hours, as well as other details such as the mission statement, the history, growth and future vision, the products and services offered, and the targeted clients, etc. The corporate profile is often used as a marketing tool to introduce the company to potential customers, investors or stakeholders, so as to advertise the company, promote business and attract investment.

Task 2: Search for the corporate profile of a company you like, e.g., KFC or Apple, through the Internet and share it with your partner. Describe what information is presented on the webpage.

Section II · *Pre-speaking*

Activity 3 Analyzing the Audience

Scan the QR code to watch a MOOC video about understanding your audience. Then read the following passage about audience analysis and complete the task that follows.

Audience Analysis

The audience members of a presentation often bring with them some background knowledge of the topic, as well as some expectations about the content of the talk. It is critical to conduct audience analysis in the preparation phase of your presentation so that your talk can successfully capture the audience's attention. For example, if you discover that the audience is very familiar with your topic, you probably should try to present something new or exciting to arouse their interests. If the audience has very little professional background about what you plan to cover, you should try to provide them with some basic knowledge and avoid difficult technical terms. In other words, the audience analysis allows the speaker to acquire relevant information about the audience, so the speaker can tailor the speech content accordingly. The analysis may involve collecting the following information:

- Demographic information: age, gender, educational level, occupation, family, etc.;
- Situational information: context, location, time, equipment availability;
- Psychological information: beliefs, values, attitudes, opinions;
- Cultural information: nationalities, cultural backgrounds;
- Interests and knowledge: priorities, interests, prior knowledge, etc.

As our lecture video points out, through audience analysis, you can find out who the listeners are, what they know, what they expect to know, what you want them to take home and what bias they have.

Now, think about Jim in Activity 2. If his presentation is delivered to a group of potential customers, you can analyze the audience by asking questions like:

- Do they know Sweet Life Snack Food Company?
- Is there any information that might interest them?
- What information would be the most interesting/important to them? (priorities)
- Do they know the various snack foods that we produce?
- Have they tried any of them?
- What might be their attitude towards the company/products?
- What are their age ranges/professions?
- Are there any products that are most popular among this age group / professional group?

- What is their income level? Will this be a factor that could influence their choice of snack foods?

When you answer these questions, you acquire a better understanding about what information to prepare for your presentation. The above are just some example questions you may ask. In fact, in your audience analysis, you may generate many other questions to obtain useful information to prepare a successful presentation.

Task: A group of investors find Sweet Life Snack Food Company quite promising and they are considering increasing their investment. They will visit the company next week before they make the final decision. Jim is asked to give a presentation to these investors. Work in pairs to help Jim conduct an audience analysis for his presentation by writing down possible answers for the questions provided in the following table and adding a few more questions you find necessary.

Questions	Answers
Who are the visitors?	*Investors, potential sponsors of the company*
What are the visitors like?	
What is the purpose of their visit?	
What do they want to find out about the company?	
Is there any information that will be particularly interesting to them?	
What is their attitude towards the company?	
What information do I want to emphasize?	

Section III *Planning*

Activity 4 Selecting Materials

Scan the QR code to watch a video about outlining the presentation and preparing the content of a corporate profile. Then read the following passage and complete the task that follows.

Selecting Materials for Business Presentations

When you are selecting materials for a business presentation, you should consider the following things:

1. Your purpose of the presentation. Why do you make the presentation? Do you want to persuade your audience to support your ideas and take actions, for example, to purchase your products, or to fund your projects? In this case, you should present compelling evidence and arguments to convince your audience. If you want to share some information about your company, you should prepare relevant facts, for instance, the corporate profile. No matter what your purpose is, you should prepare information that can help fulfill it.

2. Your audience. As we have learned, the audience's background knowledge, their interests and expectations, etc., have significant influence on the content of your talk, so such information should be considered in material selection.

3. The main points you want to convey. What are the main points you want to communicate to your audience? The material you select should be relevant to your main points, so that your talk will be coherent and logical.

4. Types of information. Consider which of the following types of information will be appropriate for your presentation: texts (handouts), statistics, images (photos, pictures, etc.), audio information (e.g., MP3 documents) and audio-visual information (movies, video clips, etc.). In fact, to achieve the best results, speakers often use more than one type of information. Also, some information may need to be processed. For example, if the text is too long and it is impossible for your audience to read all the

words, you can summarize the passage and present only the main ideas. The audience can refer to the handout afterward if they want to get the details. As for statistics, you can rearrange them in charts or tables, etc. If there are too many numbers, you can focus on the most significant ones. However, no matter how you process the information, remember that you should not distort it. Be loyal to the original information.

Task: To prepare the corporate profile presentation to a group of investors, Jim has obtained some information and materials about his company, but he is not sure what to include. Can you help him select proper information? Work with your partner and choose from the following list. Fill in the table below with appropriate number(s). Finally, explain how Jim may use the materials.

Material list:

1) Life stories of the company president Eric Smith;

2) Photos of the president and key employees of the company;

3) Photos of the company products and the manufacturing plants;

4) Photos of employee birthday parties and new year celebrations;

5) Photos of employee work scenes, employee orientation meetings and meetings with the clients;

6) A timeline of the company history and development;

7) The company's financial statements for the past 10 years;

8) Video clips of the president's speeches and TV interview scenes;

9) Key points of the company's five-year plans;

10) Video clips of the manufacturing plant and the production process;

11) Company mission statement;

12) Detailed description of some important products;

13) Photos of company branches at various locations;

14) Photos of the company when it was founded and photos of the company now;

15) Photos of some news reports about the company.

Answering table:

Purpose of the presentation: To persuade the investors that the company is worth funding.	
Audience: Any investors who want to evaluate if the company has great business prospects.	
Topics of the Presentation	**Materials Jim May Use**
Media coverage	8), 15)
General introduction	
Business development	
Key products	
Future plan	

Activity 5 Designing PPT Slides

Scan the QR code to watch a video about making visuals for a presentation. Then read the following passage and complete the task that follows.

Tips for Effective PPT Slides

Here are some tips for making effective PPT slides:

1. Organize the presentation into three parts: the introduction, body and conclusion.

2. Keep it simple. Avoid backgrounds with too many design elements: e.g., too many decorations, complex color combinations.

3. Make sure the words and the background have strong color contrast.

4. Use appropriate font size (large enough for every audience member to read easily).

5. Use empty space between the lines.

6. Include only the essential information, and avoid too many words on one slide.

7. Use tables, charts, diagrams and images to help present the information when necessary.

8. Capitalize key words in the title and the first word in a line, but do not capitalize all the letters in the words.

9. Use parallel structures.

10. Avoid overuse of special effects, e.g., animation and sound effect.

The following are two examples of effective PPT slides:

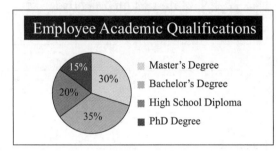

Task: Jim wanted to try different PPT designs for his presentation. He made some slides and asked Mary for advice. Each of these slides has some problems. Evaluate them and identify the drawbacks and then offer some suggestions for each slide. Scan the QR code for those PPT slides.

  **Section IV** *Practicing*

Activity 6 Using Attention-Getters

 Scan the QR code to watch a video about the structure of a presentation. Then read the first part of a passage about attention-getters and use the knowledge you have just learned to complete the task that follows.

Presenting the Introduction with an Attention-getter

A presentation consists of three parts: the introduction, body and conclusion. In the introduction section, the presenter normally uses an attention-getter to arouse the audience's interest. It could be any information that can grasp the audience's attention. Below are some commonly used attention-getters:

1. A story: Telling a short, relevant and interesting story can quickly capture the audience's attention. For example:

> Forty years ago, a little boy Eric was born in a remote village in Wyoming, US. His family was so poor that they could hardly have three square meals a day, but his parents loved him with all their hearts. They had been trying to give him their best. On the Christmas day when he was five years old, Eric got the first candy in his life. It tasted so good that Eric felt his life suddenly became sweet and beautiful. Since then, Eric has had a dream that one day, when he grew up, he would open a candy store that would bring sweetness in life and happiness to people. His dream came true 30 years later! This little boy became the president of our company, "Sweet Life Snack Food Company". As you know, our company now sells not only candies, but also plenty of other great products...

2. An amazing fact: People always enjoy things that are new, thrilling or unexpected. Using an amazing fact can instantly attract the audience's attention. For example:

> I believe you do not know that Facebook is primarily blue because Mark Zuckerberg suffers from red-green color blindness. In fact, sometimes a seemingly unrelated issue may have a significant impact on our business plan.

3. Statistics: Statistics are very effective because they provide persuasive facts and can impress the audience deeply and involve them seriously. For example:

> Each week nearly one third of the American people visit Wal-Mart and Wal-Mart makes a profit of $1.8 million every hour on average. You may wonder why Wal-Mart is so successful. Well, there are many reasons. Today, we are going to...

4. A rhetorical question: It is a question that is asked to arouse interest or draw attention rather than obtain an answer. A rhetorical question will pique the audience's curiosity and stimulate thinking; it is an interactive way to start the presentation. For example:

> Do you know that 70 percent of small businesses are actually owned and operated by only a single person? Yes! So if you want to be a business owner but are hesitating because you have no one else to help you, I have to encourage you to go ahead! It is feasible. For some great things, one person is enough.

5. A quote: People tend to value celebrities' words more. In addition, some quotes are inspiring and wisely said. Opening the presentation with a quote can grasp your

audience's attention right from the start. For example:

> Andrew Carnegie once said, "The first one gets the oyster, the second gets the shell." Does this sound familiar? Similar to the old saying, "The early bird catches the worm." Well, it may sound sad and cruel, but it is true that some fields are highly competitive and business opportunities disappear quickly. Only those with the capability and courage to act quickly will succeed. So if you have a business plan, what are you waiting for? Implement it now! Take action!

6. A description of a picture: Images are engaging because they can create vivid blueprints in the audience's mind. Using an image to start a presentation can easily involve the audience. For example:

> Please look at this picture. It shows three different designs of Coca-Cola bottles. We can see that they look quite different. Which one is the original? Why does the company change the shapes? Does the bottle design make any difference in the profits of the company?

Task: *Using an appropriate attention-getter will undoubtedly benefit your presentation introduction. Think about the following scenarios. What attention-getter would you use for each of them? Give your reasons.*

1) You are promoting the latest model of cellphones of your company to potential customers.
   _____
   _____

2) Your company is launching a research project on a product that could purify the air. You are trying to persuade some investors to fund your product development.
   _____
   _____

Unit 5 Giving a Presentation

3) You are a sales representative from a snack food company. You are introducing your products to your clients.

_____

_____

Activity 7 Delivering the Introduction

Read the second part of the passage in Activity 6 and practice delivering a full introduction part of a business speech.

    Conventionally, to start your presentation, you should first greet the audience and introduce yourself (name, position, etc.). In the introduction part of the presentation, you can exploit an attention-getter to attract the audience's attention and pique their interest. Then you present your topic and purpose of the talk. Finally, you end the introduction with an overview of the main points that will be covered. For example:

    Good morning everyone and welcome! I am Jim Johnson, the marketing director of Sweet Life Snack Food Company. I am very glad to have this opportunity to present to you today. Before I start, please taste the snacks on the plates in front of you. How do you like them? Aren't they tasty? Now you must wonder what company can produce such wonderful products. Do you want to take a guess? Yes! I know you get it. These are all products of our company. Do you want to know more about our company? Today, I would like to give you a brief introduction to our company. My talk will cover the following points: company business details and mission statement; company development timeline; company products and services; and company five-year plan.

Task: Suppose you are the marketing director of a cellphone company and will give a presentation introducing your company to some potential clients. Work with a partner and prepare the introduction part of your presentation. Make sure your introduction includes the essential elements: an interesting attention-getter, your topic and purpose, and an overview of the main points.

_____

_____

_____

Activity 8 Selecting and Arranging the Main Points

Read a passage about selecting and arranging the main points of a presentation and complete the task that follows.

Selecting and Arranging the Main Points

Order of the Main Points

The body part follows the introduction part of the presentation. In this part, you present the main points one by one, using transitions to connect the ideas. One tip for presenting the main points is to find a system to organize them. The following orders are frequently used in presentations:

1. Chronological order: You organize the information according to the time when the events happened. For example:

Topic: The development history of Power Tech Company.

Central idea: Power Tech Company has undergone three phases of development and has become the leading technology company in this country.

Main points:

a. The first phase: 2000–2005.

b. The second phase: 2006–2016.

c. The third phase: 2017–today.

2. Topical order: You organize the ideas according to different subtopics that are related to the main topic and your central idea. For example:

Topic: Marketing a product.

Central idea: Four important factors must be considered when marketing a product; these factors are called the 4 Ps of marketing.

Main points:

a. Product. First of all, you should define your product clearly and then communicate it to your consumers.

b. Price. Secondly, you should determine what price range is appropriate for your consumers and how you will balance price and quality.

c. Place. Thirdly, you should decide where to sell the products, for example, in

Unit 5 Giving a Presentation

traditional stores, through the Internet, or both.

d. Promotion. Finally, you should consider how you can convince your consumers that your product is exactly what they need.

3. Priority order: You organize the ideas according to different levels of prioritization, for example, from high level of difficulty/severity to low level, or from high level of importance to low level, or vice versa (from low to high), etc. For example:

Topic: The negative influences of COVID-19 outbreak on small businesses.

Central idea: COVID-19 outbreak has had two major negative influences on small businesses.

Main points:

a. Many businesses have been forced to close due to the COVID-19 outbreak.

b. In addition, because of the outbreak, active business activities dropped significantly, resulting in the drop of active employment.

Number of the Main Points

In the body part of the presentation, the speaker should limit the number of main points. Generally speaking, most presentations have two to three main points. Some may have four or five, but it is not a good idea to have more than five main points (Lucas, 2015)[*], because too many main points can be confusing and difficult for the audience to remember. In fact, a good strategy is to examine the main points and see whether some of the points belong to the same subtopic. If so, these points may be combined into one or organized hierarchically, one serving as the main point, and the others as supporting details.

Task: Study the following main points of the given topic and decide whether they are appropriate for a presentation outline. You are recommended to follow the reflection questions below and do some research through the Internet if necessary.

Topic: Entrepreneurs today

Central idea: Entrepreneurs today face a variety of challenges.

Main points:

1) Measuring the performance of the employees.

---

[*] Lucas, S.E. (2015). *The Art of Public Speaking*. New York: McGraw-Hill Education.

2) Hiring people who are most suitable for the job positions.

3) Advertising the products through diverse channels.

4) Delegating tasks to appropriate employees.

5) Providing satisfactory after-sales services.

6) Understanding the customers.

7) Organizing promotions.

Reflection questions:

1) Is the central idea clear and specific? If not, how can you improve it?

2) Is the number of the main points appropriate?

3) Can any of the main points listed be organized under the same subtopic? If so, how are you going to rewrite them?

4) Are there any other parts of the outline that should be improved?

Activity 9 Describing Statistics

Read the first part of a passage about describing statistics and complete the task that follows.

Statistics as Supporting Details

When presenting the main points, remember to address them one by one, using evidence to support them. Statistics are powerful supporting details because they are factual data and are objective. When using statistics, you can follow the following tips:

- Use statistics from reliable sources;
- Use visual aids (tables, charts, etc.) to clarify the statistics if necessary;
- Identify the sources of statistics;
- Round off complicated statistics (e.g., round off 13,028 to about 13,000);
- Interpret the statistics.

Task: The following PPT slide shows the statistics about the consumer age groups of a certain brand. Fill in the blanks with appropriate information to describe and explain the statistics provided on the PPT.

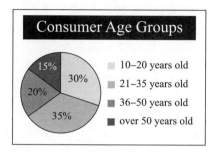

The chart shows (1) _____% of our consumers are from the age group 10–20 years old. The largest group of our consumers is from the group (2) _____; they account for (3) _____% of all consumers. The groups 36–50 and over 50 years old make up (4) _____% and (5) _____% respectively. It is evident from the statistics that our products are most (6) _____ among young people, because the (7) _____ of our consumers are below 35 years old. However, consumers aged between 35–50 and over 50 together still account for (8) _____% of our customers. Therefore, the needs of these two groups should not be (9) _____.

Activity 10 Interpreting Statistics

Read the second part of the passage in Activity 9 and complete the task that follows.

Interpreting Statistics

When using statistics to support your argument, it is not enough to simply list the numbers, because your audience may not understand what the numbers mean or what impact the statistics may have. Therefore, it is important to interpret the statistics and help the audience understand their significance. For example:

Main point: COVID-19 has had strong negative effects on small businesses in the US.

Supporting evidence:

a. Bartik et al. (2020) found that 43% of the small businesses surveyed had been temporarily closed, due to COVID-19 outbreak.

b. In addition, the businesses surveyed had reduced their active employment by 39%.

> These statistics show that because of the COVID-19 pandemic, business has shrunk severely and unemployment rate has soared, which will undoubtedly exacerbate economic insecurity and disrupt people's lives.

In the above example, the speaker adds some explanations for the statistics 43% and 39%, and makes it clear what consequences may result from the pandemic. Let's see an example again.

> In a presentation, Steve Jobs says, "We have sold four million iPhones to date. If you divide four million by two hundred days, that's twenty thousand iPhones every day on average."

This is a good example of helping the audience understand the meaning of the statistics. If Jobs simply provides the number "four million iPhones", the audience will know it is a large number, but other than that, it does not mean much because the number is put in a pretty broad context "to date", which means "to the present day". This time frame is vague and hence makes it difficult to interpret the number "four million". So for clarification, Jobs provides a specific time period "two hundred days" and adopts a smaller unit "every day", which is much clearer and more specific. Consequently, the message "twenty thousand iPhones every day on average" can be easily understood. The explanation makes the number "four million" meaningful and impressive. We should remember that statistics cannot speak for themselves; the responsibility rests on the presenter to crystallize the meaning. Therefore, as presenters, we should explain the statistics to help our audience understand them properly.

Task: Find two pieces of statistical evidence to support the following main point and interpret the statistics afterward. You may do some research through the Internet.

Main point: China's new-energy vehicle (NEV) market has been developing rapidly.

1) _____

_____

2) _____

_____

We can see that _____

_____

Unit 5 Giving a Presentation

Activity 11 Giving Examples

Read a passage about giving examples for a presentation and complete the task that follows.

Using Examples as Supporting Details

Another type of supporting evidence is examples. Examples are useful because they can help explain complicated or abstract ideas.

Let's say, you need to define the term "inflation" in your presentation. However, if you provide your audience only with the following definition from the dictionary, it is quite abstract:

> Inflation: a general rise in the prices of services and goods in a particular country, resulting in a fall in the value of money (Oxford Learners' Dictionary).

To make it easier to understand, you can explain the term again in simpler words and then give an example:

> Inflation means the same amount of money cannot buy as many things as it used to. For example, in 1913, a gallon of milk cost about 36 cents in the US. One hundred years later, in 2013, a gallon of milk cost $3.53—nearly ten times higher.

Task: Give one example to support the given topic sentence. You may use the following key words in the box to help you. Search for some source information through the Internet when preparing your example.

| after-sales service | return policy |
| free gift-wrapping service | free delivery |

Topic sentence: Customer service is highly valued in our company.

Example:

_____
_____
_____
_____

113

Activity 12 Coming to the Conclusion

Read a passage about how to conclude a presentation and complete the task that follows.

Concluding the Presentation

The last part of a presentation is the conclusion. It is the last chance for you to remind your audience of the key message you have covered in the talk. Therefore, in this part you should summarize the main points and give the presentation unity. With the summary, the audience will be more likely to remember the main ideas, even if they miss some of the body part. In addition to the summary, if you want to add more power to your conclusion, you can add a famous quote, or provide a thought-provoking or encouraging statement, etc., to create a nice closure to the presentation. For example:

> To sum up, in this presentation, I introduced four key factors of marketing, the 4 Ps of marketing, namely, product, price, place and promotion. If these four factors are clearly defined to cater to the needs of your target customers, your business will surely be successful. That's all for my presentation. Do you have any questions?

Task: Read the main part of an outline of a presentation. Then make a conclusion for the presentation by first summarizing the main points and then adding a closure to it.

Topic: The negative influence of COVID-19 outbreak on small businesses.

Central idea: COVID-19 outbreak has had two major negative influences on small businesses.

Main points:

1) Many businesses have been forced to close due to the COVID-19 outbreak.

2) In addition, because of the outbreak, active business activities dropped significantly, resulting in the drop of employment.

The conclusion part of the presentation:

_____
_____
_____
_____

Unit 5 Giving a Presentation

Activity 13 Employing Signposting Language

Read a passage about using signposting language in a presentation and complete the task that follows.

Paying Attention to Signposting Language

In an effective presentation, the speaker often uses some words or phrases to guide the audience through the talk, indicating what has been presented and what will be presented next. These words and phrases are called signposts or signposting language. Signposts can help make the presentation more coherent, better structured and easier to follow.

The following table presents some examples of signposting language:

Table 5.1   Examples of Signposting Language

Language Functions	Examples
Greeting & speech opening	● Good morning. Thanks for coming to my presentation today. ● Hello everyone! ● Good afternoon and welcome.
Introducing the topic	● The topic of my presentation is… ● Why do we use this marketing model? In this presentation, I would like to explain three reasons for our choice. ● My presentation today is about… ● Today, I will introduce an innovative approach to consumer analysis.
Giving an overview	● This presentation has three main points. First, I will define…; next, I will explain…; finally, I will comment on… ● I will start by…; after that, I will…; at the end of the presentation, I will… ● I will divide this presentation into three parts. First…; second…; third…
Presenting the main points and transitions	● I'd like to start by… ● First, I'd like to introduce… ● That's all I have to say about… Now let's look at… ● I have just explained…; next, I'd like to… ● The next issue/topic I'd like to focus on is… ● Next, let's move on to / turn to…

115

(Continued)

Language Functions	Examples
Drawing audience's attention to visuals	• As you can see from this chart... • Figure 1 shows that... • This table/graph/chart/diagram shows that...
Giving examples	• For example/instance... • Let me give you an example. • A good example of this is... • A case in point is...
Summarizing and concluding the presentation	• To sum up, in this presentation, I... • Let me briefly summarize the main points I have discussed in this presentation. • Finally, let me summarize the three main points I have covered today.

Task: Choose appropriate signposts from the expressions in the box to complete the presentation below.

Now, let me introduce our products	Today I would like to
Please feel free to ask questions	Let me begin by providing
I will mainly focus on two aspects	Good morning everyone!

(1) _____ My name is Kathy Smith. I'm the public relations director of Sweet Life Snack Food Company. Now please look at these pretty pictures of different snack foods on the slide. Have you tried these snacks before? I am sure you have. Well, as you probably know, these tasty snacks are all products of our company. In fact, I have brought some samples for you to try. Please help yourself.
(2) _____ give you a brief introduction to our company.
(3) _____: company overview and company products.

(4) _____ a brief overview of our company. Sweet Life Snack Food Company was established in September 2015 by Mr. Eric Smith. It is headquartered in New York, US. Over these years, our business has been growing very quickly. Today, we have had branches in 12 states in the US and we have worked persistently to diversify our business globally. Working with our business partners, we have sold our products to over 20 countries in the world. Our company has been devoted to adapting to the changing environment and enhancing customer

satisfaction by expanding our own unique core products, improving existing product quality and flavor, and developing diverse new snack foods. We are committed to bringing every customer safe, nutritional, tasty snack foods and enjoyable food experience. Our slogan is "Sweet Life Snack brings you sweet life".

(5) _____. Sweet Life Snack Food Company has launched diverse product lines based on extensive market research and we continue to develop new products to satisfy our consumers' needs. Currently, Sweet Life Snack Food Company has six core product lines: potato chips, chocolates, candies, mixed nuts, assorted cookies and crackers, and yogurts, with over thirty products.

OK, now I'd like to summarize what I have covered in this talk. First, I provided an overview of our company. Then, I briefly introduced our products. I believe with reliable quality, excellent taste and flavor and dedicated service, Sweet Life Snack Food Company will bring customers wonderful and exciting snack experience. That's all for my presentation. (6) _____.

Activity 14 Running the Q & A Session

Read a passage about how to run the Q & A session after a presentation and complete the task that follows.

Running the Q & A Session

Some speakers love to maintain a lively atmosphere all through the presentation and do not mind answering questions as they are presenting; others would rather not be interrupted during the presentation. No matter which approach you prefer, you'd better make it clear at the outset, i.e., in the presentation introduction. How can you address questions appropriately in presentations? Here are some tips:

- Anticipate some questions and make preparations in advance.

- After the questioner finishes asking, you should acknowledge the value of the question.

- If the question is long or complicated, check to make sure you understand correctly. You can ask clarification questions.

- If you do not know the answer, say so honestly, and then contribute some information based on what you know.

- If the question is long and complicated, divide it into a few parts and answer them separately.

- Check to make sure the question is answered properly.

Some examples are shown in the following table.

Table 5.2　Possible Situations in the Q & A Session and Useful Language Examples

Possible Situations	Examples
Telling the audience when to ask	During my presentation, please stop me if you have any questions. Please feel free (don't hesitate) to interrupt me at any time if you have questions. At the end of the presentation, there will be some time for questions. Please save your questions until the end.
Inviting questions from the audience	Now we have some time for questions. Please feel free to ask questions. I am happy to answer any questions you have. Now, do you have any questions?
Acknowledging the value of the question	● That is a great question! ● Interesting question! ● I think the point you're making is a good one. ● That's a question a lot of people have asked us recently.
Making clarification for long or complicated questions	● Do you mean…? ● Are you asking about…? ● I think you want to ask…, is that right? ● It looks like you want to ask two questions: First… Second…, Is that right?
Admitting that you don't know the answer and contributing some information based on your knowledge	● I'm not sure what…is exactly right now, but I can look that up for you later if you like. What I can tell you is that… ● That's a really interesting point and I have not thought about it. Can we discuss this after the presentation? I am sure it is worth exploring. ● That is a great point, but I have not considered it so far because it is beyond the scope of our project. We can discuss this later, because it sounds interesting. ● Sorry, I don't have a complete answer to the question right now. I will find the information and get back to you tomorrow / as soon as possible.

Unit 5 Giving a Presentation

(Continued)

Possible Situations	Examples
Checking to make sure the question is answered properly	• Does that answer your question? • Is this what you are looking for? • Do you need any more detail?

Task: Work in pairs and consider the following scenarios about running the Q & A session after a presentation. What should you do in each scenario?

1) You are going to give a 30-minute presentation about the financial status of your company. Because the information is too detailed and difficult to remember, you do not want people to interrupt you during your talk. How can you make sure this will not happen?

   _____

   _____

   _____

2) At the end of your presentation, you receive a challenging question which you have not thought about. You only have some vague ideas about it, and you need more time to find the answer. What can you do?

   _____

   _____

   _____

3) At the end of your presentation, someone asks a long and complicated question. You are not sure if you understand it correctly and do not know where to start. what can you do?

   _____

   _____

   _____

Section V   *Reflection*

Activity 15 Giving It a Try

Scan the QR code to watch a video about a company introduction. Analyze the video and complete the following tasks.

Task 1: Fill in the table below with the key elements of the corporate profile of the company MSI and share them with a partner.

Possible presenter	
Possible audience	
Possible objectives of the presentation	
Content of the presentation	

Task 2: Use the knowledge and techniques you have learned in this unit to give your own presentation on MSI to the other members of your group. Videotape your presentation for further reflection upon your delivery.

Activity 16 Mastering Delivery Skills: I

Read the first part of a passage about delivery skills and complete the task that follows.

Pausing

When speaking, you should pause properly and stress the key words. Pausing and stress can significantly enhance the comprehensibility of your presentation.

To pause means to stop briefly before you continue speaking. Pausing will give the audience time to capture the words said and to make sense of them. Proper pausing will also help the speaker convey the meaning. When should the speaker pause? In fact, they pause between thought groups. A thought group is a group of words that go together and convey a message. Each thought group contains a key word. A sentence can be divided into multiple thought groups. For example:

- Sweet Life Snack Food Company / was established / in September, / 2005.
- Headquartered in New York, US, / we have branches / in 12 states in the US.
- We manufacture and sell / a large variety of / popular snacks.

For some sentences, there may be more than one option to use thought groups and the speaker needs to decide how they would like to say it. For the following sentence, if you would like to add more emphasis to the information and speak more slowly, you may choose the second option. For example:

- Headquartered in New York, US, / we have branches / in 12 states in the US.
- Headquartered in New York, / US, / we have branches / in 12 states / in the US.

Task: Mark the thought groups where the speaker may pause in each sentence by adding a slash "/" behind each thought group.

1) The most important thing we should focus on is our current marketing project.

2) A competent employee is more productive than other employees, but this should not be used as an excuse to give more work.

3) Our company has signed a contract with JET Corporation for the construction of a shopping center.

Activity 17 Mastering Delivery Skills: II

Read the second part of the passage in Activity 16 and complete the task that follows.

Sentence Stress

Sentence stress emphasizes words that contain important content in the sentence, thus facilitating understanding by helping the audience identify the key information quickly. Generally speaking, sentence stress falls on content words, i.e., words that carry meaning. These words include: nouns, verbs, adjectives, adverbs, etc. In contrast, function words, also called grammatical words, are unstressed, because these words mainly perform grammatical functions rather than present key information. Function words include: auxiliary verbs, prepositions, articles, conjunctions, pronouns, etc. They are often unstressed. When a word is stressed, it is pronounced a little bit louder, clearer and slower, while the unstressed words are pronounced at a lower volume and higher speed. For example:

- <u>Sweet Life</u> Snack Food <u>Company</u> was <u>established</u> in <u>September, 2005</u>.
- <u>Headquartered</u> in <u>New York</u>, US, we have <u>branches</u> in <u>12</u> states in the <u>US</u>.
- We <u>manufacture</u> and <u>sell</u> a large <u>variety</u> of <u>popular snacks</u>.

It should be pointed out that you cannot stress every content word in a sentence. Instead, you should stress words that carry the meaning you want to emphasize. Therefore, stress in one sentence may vary, depending on the specific meaning the speaker wants to communicate. For example:

- The <u>manager</u> will <u>talk</u> to you **after** the <u>meeting</u>. (Emphasizes "after", not before the meeting)
- The <u>manager</u> will <u>talk</u> to **you** after the <u>meeting</u>. (Emphasizes "you", not someone else)

Task: Underline the words you will stress in the following sentences and mark the pauses in each sentence.

1) I heard the meeting is going to be canceled tomorrow.
2) So far, our products have been exported to over 20 countries in the world.
3) Marketing strategies are actions a company's management team takes to acquire new customers or retain existing ones.
4) These clients are not familiar with our company's new insurance program.

Activity 18 Using Body Language

Read a passage about using body language in a presentation and complete the task that follows.

Body Language in the Presentation

An effective presentation involves not just the content, but also the manner of delivery. It is not sufficient to just ensure a presentation has clear logic and well-organized, high-quality content; it is equally important to deliver the information in the appropriate manner. Good use of body language can make your presentation more effective. It will facilitate understanding and increase the chance that the audience will retain the information you present. Using body language means using your body parts instead of words to communicate. Body language that is useful for presentations includes:

1. Hand gestures. Do not fold your arms or close your hands when speaking. Instead, use your hands to help you identify or emphasize important information and help express your feelings or attitude.

2. Posture. Stand straight. This will make you look confident and energetic.

3. Eye contact. Face the audience and maintain eye contact with them. Look around the room so that people sitting in different places receive your attention.

4. Facial expressions. Smile. With a smile on your face, you will appear to be quite friendly and you can easily build rapport with your audience.

5. Movements. It is generally better to step out from behind the podium and face the audience. Instead of standing still, sometimes you can walk naturally on the stage. This will send the message to the audience that you are comfortable with what you are doing.

Task: Watch your own presentation video for Activity 15 and evaluate your performance with the following checklist. Then share your video with a partner and evaluate each other's video with the checklist below.

Statements	Answers
The speaker was in a standing (not sitting) position when speaking.	Yes ☐ No ☐
The speaker spoke loudly and clearly.	Yes ☐ No ☐
The speaker paused between thought groups.	Yes ☐ No ☐
The speaker used appropriate sentence stresses.	Yes ☐ No ☐
The speaker maintained eye contact with the audience.	Yes ☐ No ☐
The speaker used hand gestures effectively.	Yes ☐ No ☐
The speaker appeared confident and friendly.	Yes ☐ No ☐

Section VI Exposition

Activity 19 Conducting and Assessing the Unit Project

Get into groups. Work with your group members and do some research after class about one company you like (e.g., Huawei). Prepare a group PPT presentation about the company (about 15 minutes). Deliver the presentation to the class. Your classmates will evaluate your performance with the following scoring table. As a class, choose three excellent performing groups.

Number	Name	Total	Dimension	Score	Weight	Specifications
1			Language		20%	**Language** refers to accuracy in language use and appropriateness of word choice. **Content** concerns the relevance and sufficiency of the information provided in the company introduction. **Delivery** refers to the manner of delivering the presentation.
1			Content		40%	
1			Delivery		40%	
2			Language		20%	
2			Content		40%	
2			Delivery		40%	
3			Language		20%	
3			Content		40%	
3			Delivery		40%	
4			Language		20%	
4			Content		40%	
4			Delivery		40%	
5			Language		20%	
5			Content		40%	
5			Delivery		40%	

Unit 5 Giving a Presentation

Section VII Wrap-Up

Activity 20 Conducting Self-Evaluation

Use the following scale to self-evaluate your knowledge about giving business presentations and how well you have done in learning this unit. Four in the right column means you totally agree with each statement on the left, while zero means you totally disagree with it.

Statements	Degree of Agreement
I have known the requirements for the unit project fully.	0 1 2 3 4
I have a clear understanding of the structure of a presentation.	0 1 2 3 4
I can use an attention-getter at the beginning of the presentation.	0 1 2 3 4
I am aware of what kind of material can be used as effective supporting evidence.	0 1 2 3 4
I can incorporate statistics effectively into the presentation.	0 1 2 3 4
I have known that a PPT slide should not contain too many words.	0 1 2 3 4
I can use sentence stress and pausing naturally when presenting.	0 1 2 3 4
I have known that when I give a presentation, I should not simply read the manuscript to the audience.	0 1 2 3 4
I can organize my ideas logically in a presentation.	0 1 2 3 4
I can deliver a presentation with confidence.	0 1 2 3 4
I can run the Q & A session appropriately.	0 1 2 3 4

Module III

Developing Strategies for a New Product

Unit 6

Attending Meetings

商务职场沟通英语

  **Warm-Up**

Activity ❶ Initiating the Unit

You may have already attended some meetings in your life and are likely to attend more meetings in the future. Recall some of your experiences of attending meetings.

Task: Answer the following questions that guide you to recall the meetings you have attended before. Share your experiences with a partner. Try to use the words and phrases in the box below when necessary.

1) What kind of meetings have you ever attended?
2) When was your last meeting?
3) What was the purpose of your last meeting?
4) What was your role in the last meeting?
5) Did you have a chance to speak at the last meeting?
6) Was your last meeting successful?
7) Were you satisfied with your last meeting?
8) What needs to be improved for your last meeting?

class meeting	regular meeting	weekly team meeting
Youth League meeting	information sharing meeting	decision-making meeting
problem-solving meeting	team-building meeting	status upgrade meeting
idea-generating meeting	chairperson	participant/attendee
punctual/unpunctual	efficient/inefficient	lack of participation
lack of time management	no clear goal	no clear takeaway

Unit 6 Attending Meetings

Activity 2 Understanding the Key Concept

Read an office conversation where some sales team members are talking about preparing for a team meeting. Read the conversation in pairs and complete the task that follows.

Linda: Hey guys, I sent you the **agenda** of the weekly meeting to your email box this morning. Do you have any feedback? Paul, what do you think?

Paul: Yeah. I must admit the purpose of the meeting is quite clear. Yes, we need some discussion about the solution to increase our sales in the next season. However, as far as I know, low staff morale in some outlets seems to be spreading. Should we give it a priority in our meeting?

Linda: Absolutely. But who can tell us what's going on there?

Frank: Maybe we should invite Tina Anderson from the HR Department to the meeting. She recently finished her survey on staff morale in the major outlets. I mean we can listen to her opinion first.

Linda: Good idea, Frank. I'll email her later. If her time permits, we'll kick off our meeting with Tina, and then try to find out specific connections between low staff morale and sales decrease.

Task: Explain what an agenda is in your own words.

_____

_____

You can check the reference here.

Knowledge Notes

An agenda contains a list of topics in the order of priority that the participants of a meeting expect to discuss, or a series of issues that they need to address. With an agenda, a meeting will have a clear goal and, therefore, can be more productive. In addition, if all the items are expected to be covered within a meeting, the agenda will also be a time management and pace control tool.

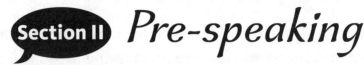

Activity 3 Summarizing Meeting Objectives

Study the first part of a meeting conversation below and complete the task that follows.

> **Linda:** Okay. Can we start right now, please? The main purpose of today's meeting is to find out what has caused a dramatic loss of morale within the sales force in three of our major outlets.
>
> **The Others:** Yes.
>
> **Linda:** I'd like to kick off the meeting with a presentation by Tina Anderson from the HR Department. Tina has just finished a survey on the company's staff morale as a whole. I think she has something to tell us. After her presentation, we'll discuss what we can do to solve the problem. Finally, we will leave the meeting with takeaways, including your assignment and deadline. Now, Tina please.
>
> **Tina:** Well. Thanks, Linda. Thanks for having me. My presentation will try to focus on the sales teams in the three outlets. I will mainly offer you some facts about what was going on in the last three months, but I won't give you any suggestions for improving the situation there. Just feel free to raise questions whenever you want.
>
> **The Others:** Okay. Get it.
>
> **Tina:** Here we go. It started half a year ago. My colleagues and I got some complaints from one of our sales teams. They attacked that the design of our customer satisfaction scoring system was unacceptable. Specifically, because the system encourages customers to evaluate the sales service even during the cooling-off period, customers may use the evaluation right as a bargaining chip to obtain extra discounts. If the salesperson does not have the authority to approve the discounts, they will be scored unkindly, resulting in invalid ratings. We...

Unit 6 Attending Meetings

Tracy: At what scale does this happen? Are they only some sporadical cases?

Tina: Not exactly. I will talk about it soon later.

Linda: Tracy, let Tina continue please.

Tracy: Okay. No problem.

Tina: We investigated this issue and found that it happens when...

Task: Answer the two questions below. Write down the purpose of the meeting in the blank and complete an infographic that summarizes the meeting objectives.

1) What is the purpose of the meeting?

_____

_____

2) What are the main objectives of the meeting? Complete the infographic below.

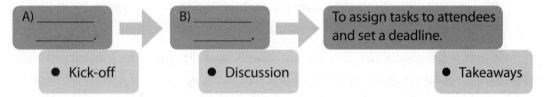

| A) _____ _____. | B) _____ _____. | To assign tasks to attendees and set a deadline. |

- Kick-off
- Discussion
- Takeaways

Activity 4 Identifying the Roles

Analyze the above meeting in Activity 3 and complete the following task.

Task: Write down the roles of each participant of the meeting in the table below. You should use the phrases provided in the box.

Linda's Roles	Tina's Roles	Tracy's Roles
•	•	•
•	•	•
•	•	•

133

interrupting with questions	stating the aim
inviting for a formal talk	sharing ideas
giving clarification	coordinating the participants
keeping the meeting on the track	

Activity 5 Distinguishing Meetings from Group Discussions

Read a passage about the connections and differences between meetings and group discussions. Then complete the task that follows.

Meetings vs. Group Discussions

Although a group discussion is an inevitable session of a meeting, or a type of meeting itself, it differs from formal meetings in a number of ways.

At first, a group discussion may not have a specific goal. The participants just exchange ideas and opinions around a particular topic. And it's not a must for them to reach any agreements or make any decisions. Therefore, a group discussion emphasizes the process over result.

Secondly, in a group discussion, there is no need to guide participants to cover a series of topics one after another according to the prescribed time. However, the chairperson of a meeting is responsible for facilitating the meeting to progress in line with the agenda and managing the meeting to finish on time.

Last but not least, all group members have the chance to speak spontaneously in a group discussion. They can express their ideas more freely, exchange their thoughts more frankly, and communicate with each other more equally. In contrast, the group leader often takes the lead in the meeting in Chinese culture.

Task: Complete the following summary table by filling in each blank with one word from the above passage. You can change the word form to make the context cohesive and coherent.

Unit 6 Attending Meetings

Points	Group Discussion	Meeting
1	It can be relatively casual. There is no need to achieve the (1) _____.	It is usually formal. It needs to end with a(n) (2) _____.
2	It goes freely and ends naturally. It proceeds without time (3) _____.	It needs tight control. Its topic follows the (4) _____ and its time is fixed.
3	It allows all members to speak more freely, exchange ideas more (5) _____, and communicate with each other more equally.	It is highly organized in Chinese meetings by a more authoritative person who usually takes the (6) _____ in the process.

Activity 6 Understanding the Unit Project

Read the rubric about the unit project below. Then have a quick discussion with other group members to make sure you understand the project fully.

Background Information:

WearWise is a small company based in a Chinese city. It specializes in wearables with hi-tech materials. It has recently developed a kind of waterproof cloth called the Lotus Leaf. It is oil, moisture, smear, dust and chemical resistant. The textile of the Lotus Leaf is a thin, soft and comfortable fabric. It is also a good insulator.

The Lotus Leaf can be used to develop many new products, such as waterproof clothes, umbrellas, phone cases, etc.

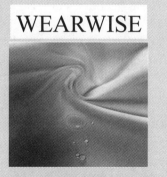

Selling Points:

- The phone case is very light.
- It comes in many colors.
- It does not generate static electricity.
- It is water, oil, smear, dust and chemical resistant.
- It fluoresces at night.

Task: Hold a group meeting to design a prototype product using the Lotus Leaf. Your new product can be waterproof clothes, umbrellas, phone cases, or anything innovative. During your meeting, you should discuss about and decide on the following questions.

1) What kind of product do you want to design by using the Lotus Leaf?
2) What is the name of your new product?
3) What are the main characteristics of the product? (selling points)
4) What are the advantages of your product over its competitors?
5) Who will probably buy your product? (the target customers)
6) At what price can the product attract the buyers?
7) Where can the product be sold to the buyers? (the outlets)

Don't start the meeting until you proceed to Activity 13 where you will read more requirements. Before you can handle the meeting, you should finish learning more meeting skills by following a series of activities.

Section III *Planning*

Activity 7 Writing an Agenda

Scan the QR code to watch a video about how to write an agenda. Then read a passage about the same topic and complete the task that follows.

As we have mentioned in Activity 2, an agenda is a step-by-step outline for participants to follow in a meeting. However, designing an agenda is not the same as drawing a time table or a process chart. In this part, you will go further to learn how to write an agenda for a business team meeting.

1. Meeting Information

Your meeting should have a straightforward name, as well as a specific date, time and location. Then, the meeting convenor, attendees and absentees should be put down. Next, your agenda should state the meeting objectives clearly and briefly. The more clarity you can offer on the goals of the meeting, the more likely you will be to achieve them efficiently. If meeting documents need to be kept as archives in line with corporate file management, the agenda should be given a code number.

2. Meeting Preparation

For a more efficient and productive meeting, participants should do their homework beforehand. They are expected to read the documents sent out with the agenda. What's more, the agenda can also be used as a reminder for the participants who will be responsible for the keynote talks or presentations.

3. Meeting Topics / Action Items

The arrangement of topics or action items is the main part of an agenda. A table can be employed to specify the main points of each topic or action item, the presentation to spark a discussion that follows, the presenter and duration of the presentation, and estimated duration of the discussion. It is a good way to break down the topics to points by asking specific supporting questions. And it is wise not to pack too many topics in the agenda and it is realistic to pre-set adequate time to have meaningful discussions, Q & A sessions and to agree on the follow-up actions.

4. Meeting Adjournment

At the end of your agenda, state clearly at what time your meeting will be closed.

Task: You are provided with a template below that illustrates the format of an agenda. Create your own agenda for the project meeting assigned in Activity 6 with the help of the template.

Meeting Agenda

Meeting Code:

Name:
Date:
Time:
Location:

Objectives:

___

Convenor:
Attendees:
Absentees:
Keynote speakers / presenters:
Invited guests:

___

Last meeting minutes:

___

Topics/Action Items:

Topic 1	Point 1: Point 2: Point 3:	
Action 1	1. Having a presentation on the issue 2. Discussing for problem and cause analysis 3. Summarizing	Presenter: _____ Duration: _____ (min) Duration: _____ (min) Duration: _____(min)
Topic 2	Point 1: Point 2: Point 3:	
Action 2	1. Discussing for resolutions 2. Summarizing 3. Agreeing on follow-up actions	Duration: _____ (min) Duration: _____ (min) Duration: _____ (min)

___

Adjournment:

Unit 6 Attending Meetings

Activity 8 Reaching an Agreement

When your agenda is done, you should email it to all the participants to make sure the topics or action items you selected are relevant to everyone. By doing this, you may know whether you have missed any important matters or not. If you want your meeting to engage every teammate and achieve as much as you expect, do ask for feedback from others.

Task: Email the agenda to every other participant or have a face-to-face group discussion to collect feedback on the agenda and revise it until the agenda is accepted by all of you.

Section IV *Practicing*

Activity 9 Mastering Functional Utterances

Meeting speech contains a variety of functional utterances that serve specific purposes.

Tasks: You are provided with some meeting utterances and their functions. Match each utterance with its function.

For the chairperson:

Functions	Utterances
1) Setting objectives	A) Bob, before the next meeting, I want the data analysis completed, so that we can discuss the results.
2) Closing an item	B) I'll have to keep each item to 20 minutes. Otherwise we'll never get through.

(Continued)

Functions	Utterances
3) Speeding up	C) Before we close, let me just go over the main points.
4) Suggesting a vote	D) If nobody has anything to add, let's move on to the next item.
5) Stating a future action	E) Since we can't get a unanimous decision, I suggest we vote on item 3.
6) Summarizing	F) We're here today to discuss the progress of the ABC project.

For other participants:

Functions	Utterances
1) Keeping the meeting on the track	A) That's an excellent point, but I'd like to differ.
2) Disagreeing politely	B) From my perspective, it's a little more complicated. Let me explain.
3) Making suggestions/proposals	C) Sorry, just to be clear, do you mean it will lead to negative outcomes?
4) Interrupting politely	D) I'm afraid that's outside the scope of this meeting. Why don't we return to the agenda?
5) Dealing with interruptions	E) Can we come back to that point later? Let me just finish what I was saying.
6) Clarifying	F) I understand your approach fully, but can we discuss some other alternatives?

Activity 10 Practicing Functional Utterances

You are provided with three short office conversations below. Imagine you are one of the speakers of each conversation and complete the conversation with your own utterances.

Task: Fill in the blanks with your own utterances to make the following conversations complete and coherent. Your utterances should also be appropriate in the context and effective to fulfill the speakers' purposes.

Unit 6 Attending Meetings

Conversation 1

Daniel: Have you all received a copy of the agenda? Good. Shall we start with the first item?

(1) _____?

Henry: Okay. Thanks Daniel. Before I start my presentation about the project plan, please allow me to ask you a question.

Conversation 2

Peter: I suggest we fix our launching date in October because there is a gap in the market.

Rebecca: (2) _____?

Peter: I mean that according to the market's need analysis, there is an increasing demand of new energy vehicles because of the National Day holiday. And our major competitor will not launch their latest model early than November.

Conversation 3

Teresa: Hold on a minute. I think we are talking about the product's package color, not about pricing it.

Martin: You're right, Teresa.

(3) _____.

Activity 11 Writing Meeting Minutes

Scan the QR code to watch a video about the essentials of meeting minutes. Then read a passage about the same topic and complete the task that follows.

What Is Meeting Minutes and How to Write It

As a written report of a meeting, the minutes document and highlight the key issues discussed, motions proposed, agreements voted on, activities to be undertaken and responsibilities to be assumed. A secretary or a member of the group will be designated to take the minutes.

Although minutes writing usually needs to transcribe the audio or video meeting records, it is unnecessary to take down every single word. Overall, the minutes of a team meeting basically include the following details:

- Basic information about the meeting: date, time, location, etc.;
- Names of attendees and absentees;
- Approval of agenda and minutes of the previous meeting;
- Decisions made about each agenda item, such as:
  - Motions accepted or rejected;
  - Actions agreed upon;
  - Follow-up actions related to every member;
  - Items postponed or suspended for further consideration;
  - Voting outcomes.
- Addition to agenda (if necessary);
- Adjournment;
- Date and time of the next meeting (if necessary);
- Minutes taker's auto-signature.

Within 24 hours after the meeting, the minutes are supposed to distribute to all the other members and facilitators as well.

Task: Judge whether the following statements about minutes writing are true (T) or false (F) based on what you have just learned.

1) Meeting minutes are the transcripts of what happened in a meeting. (   )

2) Meeting minutes should respond to and echo the agenda items one after another. (   )

3) Decisions include motions and actions that are agreed upon, while excluding rejected ones. (   )

4) Postponed and rejected agenda items shouldn't be included in the minutes. (   )

5) The minutes should be written and distributed to the others as soon as possible. (   )

Unit 6 Attending Meetings

Activity 12 Completing Meeting Minutes

You are provided with the second part of the meeting conversation in Activity 3, followed by the incomplete minutes. You should complete the minutes with the information in the conversation below.

Linda: Thanks Tina. Thank you for your presentation. Before we can discuss for resolutions, please allow me to summarize Tina's main points in a few seconds. Why is there low morale within about 30% of our sales force in three of our major outlets? In a nutshell, nearly one tenth of the salespeople complain that their customers use the satisfaction scoring system to demand extra discounts either within or after the cooling-off period, and that about one third of them are badly rated simply because they don't have the authority to approve the expected price. On the other hand, because more salespeople who get low scores for three consecutive months are laid off, the increasing turnover has led to the lack of well-experienced salespeople in these outlets. The situation is really tough and our mission is to stop the decrease of sales in the next season. So, do you have anything to say?

Paul: I think there is at least one thing we can do immediately—stop scoring within the cooling-off period.

Tracy: Yes, I agree. Customers will become more rational in this way.

Frank: Can we be more realistic? I mean we can't look for solutions from the customer. We should take back the power of offering normal discounts from the sales force. By doing this, customer satisfaction will no longer be decided by how much discount the customer can obtain. That'll be fair to everyone.

Tracy: What about flexibility? If the salespeople can't capture customers by using quick incentives for a short time, we will lose customers.

Paul: Frank, it is not in our long-term interest to have over-centralized sales teams.

Linda: I prefer a compromise here. Can we lower the normal discount to 5%? If the customer wants a larger one, the salesperson needs to be authorized to offer that discount from the team supervisor. I hope this approach will help resist the impact of using discounts as incentives to obtain high customer satisfaction scores.

Frank: Sounds acceptable to me.

Paul and Tracy: Me too.

Linda: Okay. Then, let's shift to the second issue. How can we deal with the problem of needing more well-experienced salespeople in these outlets?

Tracy: First, we can dispatch some experienced salespeople to the three outlets from other stores. Second, we can give more training to the newly-recruited green hands.

Paul: I can't agree more. Our training program is trustworthy.

Frank: And I think regular team building meetings to develop a rapport will help the new salespeople to communicate better.

Linda: Great. Everyone seems confident in fixing the problems. So, here comes our final topic...

Task: Complete the following unfinished minutes with the information in the above conversation.

Meeting Minutes

May 8th, 2023

Code Number: MT2208085

Opening

The regular meeting of Marketing Department was called to order at 14:30 on May 8th, 2023 in the department meeting room 403.

Present

Linda Hall, Head of Sales

Paul Walker, Senior Sales Executive

Frank Jones, Sales Executive

Tracy Taylor, Sales Executive

Tina Anderson, Senior HR Executive

Unit 6 Attending Meetings

Absent

   None.

Approval of Agenda

   The agenda of this meeting was unanimously approved as distributed.

Approval of Minutes

   The minutes of the previous meeting were unanimously approved as distributed.

Report

   A report about the causes of low staff morale in three major outlets was presented by Tina Anderson. The causes are:

   1) Nearly one tenth of the salespeople complained that their customers had used the satisfaction scoring system to demand extra discounts either within or after the cooling-off period. And about one third of those salespeople received bad ratings simply because they had no authority to approve the expected price.

   2) The increasing turnover has led to the lack of well-experienced salespeople in the three major outlets.

Motions

   About salespeople's complaint:

   1) _____ (Rejected)

   2) _____ (Rejected)

   3) _____ (Accepted)

   About salespeople's turnover:

   1) _____ (Accepted)

   2) _____ (Accepted)

Adjournment

   The meeting was adjourned at 15:10 by Linda Hall. The next meeting will be held at 14:30 on June 5th, 2023.

Minutes submitted by: *Linda Hall*

Activity 13 Giving It a Try

Now, you can hold the group meeting to come up with the prototype design stated in Activity 6. Before the meeting, you should decide who will be the chairperson and who will be the participants. And you should also review the agenda you have set in Activity 7 and Activity 8. While you are attending the meeting, you should get engaged and try to employ the functional utterances you have learned. When your group meeting is being held, another group will come to observe and comment on your meeting performance by using the following checklist. You should videotape the group meeting to facilitate the peer review.

Questions	Answers
Has the meeting group prepared an agenda?	Yes ☐ No ☐
Is the agenda highly relevant to Activity 6?	Yes ☐ No ☐
Is the agenda design qualified?	Yes ☐ No ☐
What's your comment on the agenda design?	The well-done: _____ The shortcomings: _____
Has the agenda been distributed to all the participants?	Yes ☐ No ☐
Has the agenda been approved by all the participants?	Yes ☐ No ☐
Can the chairperson use functional utterances appropriately?	Yes ☐ No ☐
Is the chairperson good at organizing the meeting?	Yes ☐ No ☐
What's your comment on the chairperson's job?	The well-done: _____ The shortcomings: _____
Can the participants use functional utterances appropriately?	Yes ☐ No ☐
Are the participants actively engaged during the meeting?	Yes ☐ No ☐
What's your comment on the participants' performance?	The well-done: _____ The shortcomings: _____

Unit 6 Attending Meetings

(Continued)

Questions	Answers
Have all the meeting objectives been accomplished?	Yes ☐ No ☐
Do all the participants clearly know their follow-up actions?	Yes ☐ No ☐
Will all the participants receive the meeting minutes?	Yes ☐ No ☐
What's your comment on the adjournment of the meeting?	The well-done: _____ The shortcomings: _____

 *Reflection*

Activity 14 Improving Awkward Utterances

You are provided with an excerpt from the transcript of a students' group meeting. In the excerpt, there are some underlined parts representing some problems with the appropriateness of speaking. The problems and their reflecting questions and explanations are also provided for you beneath the conversation.

Chairperson: OK. Now we can go into our third part—(to) review our original product design and make some modifications. Who has any ideas?

Participant 1: [Problem 1] <u>We can, we can have some different prices for our product to suit different people</u>. [Porblem 2] <u>And</u> we can have just convenient and comfortable (price) for some person, <u>and</u> have a higher (price) product for another person.

Participant 2: [Problem 3] <u>I think the hidden charge access is our product's selling</u>

point. Because nowadays, almost every charge access is left uncovered. If we can hide it, the phone case can cover the phone completely to show a symmetric look. I think if we want to, if we want to compete with other products, we can, we can show this innovative design characteristic.

Chairperson: OK, thank you. [Problem 4] <u>Anyone else has opinions about the shape of our phone case? No? No one?</u> Then, we're going to our final part—(to) make sure our design and make a brief summary. First, we need to make sure (what) our product is like. So, I'll repeat our conclusion, some modifications about our original design. I think we can save some, save some..., I mean, we can just divide our product into different parts. No, not parts, different classes for different people. [Problem 5] <u>All in all, just different designs for different persons.</u> I think this is our main idea, right?

Task: Study the problems and their explanations below, and then improve them by replacing the underlined parts with more appropriate expressions.

Problem 1

> **Reflecting question:** Does Participant 1 talk about modifications of product design or product pricing?
>
> **Explanation:** The participants should keep the meeting on track. The discussion should follow the agenda, proceeding from the items with the highest priority to less important ones.

Your improvement:

_____

_____

Problem 2

> **Reflecting question:** Do the two words of "and" mean what they should mean?
>
> **Explanation:** Appropriate linking/signal words should be used to express ideas more precisely. The first "and" is an alternative statement of the previous sentence, while the second "and" actually means a contrast.

Your improvement:

_____

_____

Problem 3

Reflecting question: Does Participant 2 seem to be abrupt when he/she takes the turn to speak?

Explanation: When a participant needs to take the conversation turn, he/she is expected to speak around the on-going topic. If he/she wants to shift the topic, start with a short comment on the previous speaker's ideas. Don't start a new topic directly. No speaker wants to be ignored by the others.

Your improvement:

_____

_____

Problem 4

Reflecting question: Should the chairperson drop an agenda item if nobody wants to speak about it?

Explanation: When the meeting falls in silence, it's the chairperson's responsibility to find a way to break the ice. Try to change the way of asking questions, such as zooming in the focus or shrinking from general to more specific concerns. Don't just skip to another agenda item unless you want it to happen as a strategy.

Your improvement:

_____

_____

Problem 5

Reflecting question: Does the chairperson's summary include every main point?

Explanation: When the chairperson delivers the meeting summary, he/she should include all the important ideas and decisions related to the agenda items. Besides, the chairperson should be certain about what needs to be summarized and should speak in a more organized way.

Your improvement:

_____

_____

Activity 15 Reflecting on Delivery Skills

Study the delivery rules of public talk in the Appendix (on Page 203). Then work in a group to find out your delivery problems in the videotapes of your group meeting in Activity 13. And finally, discuss how to improve your delivery skills for meetings. Some guiding questions are provided for you below.

1) In general, can you successfully grab the audience's attention and clearly convey your ideas?
2) Is the volume of your voice at an appropriate level?
3) Do you sometimes change your pitch to direct the audience's attention to your information?
4) Do you sometimes slow down or speed up to convey different purposes?
5) Do you sometimes intentionally pause for some special purposes?
6) Do you sit straight in a natural way and avoid shaking your legs?
7) Do you have natural facial expressions to show your confidence and professionalism?
8) Do you have eye contact with each of your teammates briefly from time to time?
9) Do you use gestures spontaneously and naturally?
10) Do you pay attention to the reaction and feedback of your audience and adjust the way you talk?

Section VI *Exposition*

Activity 16 Conducting and Assessing the Unit Project

Hold a second group meeting in this exposition activity. The new meeting involves a session of presenting the results of a market survey, which will be instructed in Unit 7. In view of that, this activity should be held up till you proceed to Activity 15 of Unit 7. However, the rubric of this activity is still stated here. The new group meeting needs to (1) familiarize the participants with the market's feedback on the customers' satisfaction of your preliminary product design done in the first meeting, and (2) discuss solutions to fix the design.

Once again, a peer-review group will observe your group meeting and evaluate your performance. The peer-review group should use the scoring table below to evaluate the group meeting under observation. It is necessary for the assessing group to negotiate an agreement on the final scores. The scoring table can also be replicated for individual scoring. In this case, the mean score for every dimension should be added up as the final result.

Product Design	Dimension	Score	Weight	Specifications
Agenda (10%)	Language		5%	**Language** refers to accuracy in pronunciation, grammar, coherence; and appropriateness of word choice and functions. **Content** concerns the quality of the products, including what elements and structure they should have, how detailed and informative they are and whether the meeting has covered all the agenda items. **Delivery** means how skillfully and intentionally the verbal and non-verbal techniques can be used to achieve the purposes.
	Content		5%	
Presentation (30%)	Language		10%	
	Content		10%	
	Delivery		10%	
Meeting (40%)	Language		15%	
	Content		15%	
	Delivery		10%	
Minutes (20%)	Language		10%	
	Content		10%	
Total score: _____			Anything else: _____	

Section VII Wrap-Up

Activity 17 Conducting Self-Evaluation

Use the following scale to self-evaluate your knowledge about holding and attending meetings and how well you have done in learning this unit. Four in the right column means you totally agree with each statement on the left, while zero means you totally disagree with it.

Statements	Degree of Agreement
I have known the requirements for the unit project fully.	0　1　2　3　4
I have known my roles in the group meetings very well.	0　1　2　3　4
I have prepared for the meetings very well.	0　1　2　3　4
I can fully understand the presentation in meetings.	0　1　2　3　4
I can use functional language in meetings.	0　1　2　3　4
I can fully understand what others say in meetings.	0　1　2　3　4
I can use delivery skills in meetings.	0　1　2　3　4
I have experienced successful meetings.	0　1　2　3　4
I have mastered how to set an agenda for meetings.	0　1　2　3　4
I have gained much experience for business meetings.	0　1　2　3　4
I have greatly improved my communication skills.	0　1　2　3　4
I have become less anxious when I attend meeting discussions.	0　1　2　3　4
I have mastered how to write minutes for meetings.	0　1　2　3　4

Unit 7

Conducting a Market Survey

  Warm-Up

Activity 1 Initiating the Unit

After designing a prototype product in Unit 6, you need to get some feedback on it from the market, e.g., who the target customers are; what the market potential is; which selling point is the most valuable; and what sales channel is ideal. Familiarize yourselves with the key terms listed below.

Task: Match each term with its explanation.

1) target customers
2) market potential
3) selling points
4) sales channels

a) The features that differentiate your product or service from that of your competitors.
b) The outlets or shops a business uses to sell a product or service.
c) People identified as the most likely to purchase a company's product or service.
d) The evaluation of the sales volume expected from a product or service.

Activity 2 Understanding the Key Concept

John is the R & D manager of Xcres, a smart watch manufacturer. When having morning tea, John and his friend Joe have a casual conversation about using a market survey to gain insight into a new product's market potential. Read the conversation in pairs and complete the task that follows.

Joe: Hi, John. You look tired. What's up?

John: I had a long meeting with my team, trying to work out the key features of the new

Unit 7 Conducting a Market Survey

product we are developing.

Joe: Sounds interesting! What are the key features?

John: Well, I cannot tell you that!

Joe: All right. But how can you know whether your customers like the new product with those key features?

John: Good question! We test them.

Joe: Test them? How?

John: We work with a market research company to conduct a **market survey** with our target customers. Then we get information about lots of things, like what features they like or dislike, and to what extent.

Joe: Brilliant! I wish you all the best for the new product development.

Task: Explain what a market survey is in your own words.

_____

_____

You can check the reference here.

Knowledge Notes

A market survey is a tool to directly investigate into the market for a particular product or service. It collects feedback from the target audience to understand the consumers' buying potential, including their characteristics, expectations, requirements, attitudes and preferences.

商务职场沟通英语

Section II Pre-writing

Activity 3 Applying the Key Terms

After the meeting, John is having a network video conference with Lee, a consultant from a market research company. They work together to brainstorm critical issues about the market survey regarding how the survey questionnaire should be designed and distributed. Read the following conversation and complete the task that follows.

John: This survey questionnaire aims to test how our (1) _____ feel about the new product we are developing, so we can predict its (2) _____.

Lee: So the first few items should help locate your target customers, and the main thing about the questionnaire is to see if they like the key features, or in other words, the (3) _____ of the new watch.

John: Right! Can we also gain some information about where they want to buy the smart watch, such as the shopping malls and online stores?

Lee: You mean the (4) _____?

John: Yes. That's important for us to achieve our marketing objectives.

Lee: Sure. Then how do you want to (5) _____ this survey questionnaire? I suggest using some (6) _____ platforms, like Weibo, WeChat, Xiaohongshu, and Bilibili, as your target customers are mainly 80s and younger. If you also target the international market, we can consider using Facebook, Instagram, and Twitter.

John: That's a good idea. We can also send a(n) (7) _____ to those customers who have registered as our members.

Task: Fill in the blanks with the appropriate forms of the words or phrases in the box below.

sales channel	distribute	email	market potential
target customer	social media	selling point	

Activity 4 Deciding the Target Audience and Distribution Channels

Run-fast, a Chengdu-based shoe manufacturer, is developing a new product line, a sneaker that can change its color as the wearer's body temperature rises. To gain some feedback from the potential market, Run-fast plans to conduct a market survey through questionnaires.

Task: Discuss with your partner the following questions that may be critical to a successful survey.

1) Who are the target audiences? Can you describe the main characteristics of the survey respondents, such as their gender, age, income, profession, etc.?

   _____

   _____

2) How do you plan to distribute the questionnaire (e.g., email, social media, website, a QR code on places where people can scan and access the questionnaire link through a mobile phone, such as a receipt) and why?

   _____

   _____

Activity 5 Sampling Respondents

Read a passage about survey sampling and complete the task that follows.

When conducting market research, it is not practical to include every one of your target population. This means the responses collected from a small group of that population need to accurately reflect the characteristics (e.g., views, behaviour) of the larger population you target. For example, if your target population is 1,000 customers of a product or service, among which 60% are male and 40% are female, then your samples must also reflect this ratio of gender.

Task: The pie chart below shows the initial analysis of the market survey that aims to understand how 1,000 customers feel about the Run-fast sneakers. The male to female gender ratio is 3:1. Discuss with a partner whether the sampled respondents reflect the gender ratio of the target population and why.

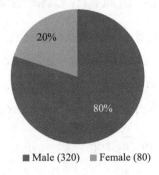

Figure 7.1 Gender of the respondents

I think _____

_____

Section III Planning

Activity 6 Understanding the Questionnaire Structure

Read a passage about the structure of a market survey questionnaire and complete the task that follows.

  A complete market survey questionnaire usually consists of five sections: (1) introduction—introduces some basic information about the market survey, so the respondents would know what the survey is about and what they are supposed to do; (2) screening/filtering section—question(s) that either qualify or disqualify respondents, thus to make sure that the respondents meet the survey criteria; (3) the section for biographic information—questions collecting respondents' personal information; (4) the main section—the core part, which can be further divided into sections addressing different objectives, such as surveying the attitude towards the main features of the product, profiling the target customers and/or testing pricing strategies and sales channels; (5) conclusion and thank-you—a sentence or two at the end of your questionnaire, or a follow-up thank-you page, indicating completion of the questionnaire and expressing gratitude to the respondents for their time.

Task: Read the sample questionnaire on the left and fill in the blanks on the right with the words or phrases in the box below.

Thank you for purchasing Run-fast products. We're conducting a short survey to find out about your shopping experience and what we may do to improve our service. Please complete the questionnaire and send it back to survey@newstar.com. Customers who complete the questionnaire will get a $10 voucher.
Q1. Are you
    A. Male.
    B. Female.
	1) The first paragraph is a(n) _____.

Q2. What is your age?
    A. Under 20.
    B. 21–30.
    C. 31–40.
    D. 41–50.
    E. 51–60.
    F. Over 60.
…
	2) Q1 and Q2 are collecting _____.

Q5. How many times have you purchased Run-fast products in the last 6 months?
    A. Never.
    B. Fewer than 3 times.
    C. 4–6 times.
    D. More than 6 times.
…
	3) Q5 is a(n) _____ question.

Q8. Overall, how satisfied are you with your most recent buy from Run-fast?
    A. Extremely satisfied.
    B. Somewhat satisfied.
	4) Q8 to Q15 are _____.

C. Neither satisfied nor dissatisfied.
D. Somewhat dissatisfied.
E. Extremely dissatisfied.

Q9. Based on your most recent shopping experience, how likely are you to purchase our products again?
A. Extremely likely.
B. Very likely.
C. Moderately likely.
D. Slightly likely.
E. Not at all likely.

…

Q15. Do you have any additional comments? If so, please enter them below.

This completes our questionnaire. Thank you for your time.

5) The last paragraph is _____.

---

biographic information   introduction   screening/filtering
the main section   conclusion and thank-you

Activity 7 Identifying Appropriate Items

After locating the target customers and deciding the distribution of the survey, Run-fast is now developing the questionnaire items through an online tool. Read a passage about different types of questionnaire items and complete the task that follows.

There are generally two broad categories of questionnaire questions, or more precisely items: close-ended and open-ended.

Close-ended items usually have a pre-defined list of answer options, which can be further divided into three types: (1) dichotomous questions—they offer only two options for the respondents to choose between, such as the True/False and Yes/No questions. With clear-cut options, this type of question is easy to answer and often appears at the start; (2) multiple choice questions—they offer a variety of options, allowing the respondents to select only one or more options. It is easy for the respondents to fill out and provide clean data for analysis; (3) scales—they display a scale of options from any range, such as 1 to 5, 1 to 10, or from "Strongly agree" to "Strongly disagree", from "Not at all likely" to "Extremely likely". This type of question is usually used to measure opinions, attitudes, etc.

Open-ended items ask respondents to provide an answer in their own words, which is expected to offer more details.

Task: Consider whether the following questionnaire items are appropriate for the given purposes, and then give your opinion to your partner. An example has been given.

Purpose 1: Understand to what extent the customers are satisfied with our service

Questionnaire Items	Judgments and Reasons
1) Are you satisfied with our service? A) Yes. B) No.	*This item is not appropriate, because it is a dichotomous question and cannot show the extent.*
2) I am satisfied with your service. A) True. B) False.	
3) How satisfied are you with our service? A) Extremely satisfied. B) Somewhat satisfied. C) Neither satisfied nor dissatisfied. D) Somewhat dissatisfied. E) Extremely dissatisfied.	
4) Please indicate your level of agreement or disagreement with the following statements.<table><tr><th>Statements</th><th>Strongly Disagree</th><th>Disagree</th><th>Neutral</th><th>Agree</th><th>Strongly Agree</th></tr><tr><td>Score</td><td>1</td><td>2</td><td>3</td><td>4</td><td>5</td></tr><tr><td>The staff are friendly.</td><td></td><td></td><td></td><td></td><td></td></tr><tr><td>The service is excellent.</td><td></td><td></td><td></td><td></td><td></td></tr></table>	

Purpose 2: Understand why the customers like our service

Questionnaire Items	Judgments and Reasons
5) Which of the following do you like about our service? A) We respond quickly. B) We are available 24/7. C) We offer good service at a competitive price. D) Our staff are friendly. E) Others. (Offer your answer in the box below.)	
6) Can you talk about the main reasons you choose to purchase our service? (Offer your answer in the box below.)	

Activity 8 Outlining Your Questionnaire for the Unit Project

WearWise is a small company based in China. It has recently produced a new waterproof material called the Lotus Leaf. Your group has designed a prototype product using the Lotus Leaf in Unit 6. In order to get some feedback on the prototype from the market, your group needs to conduct a market survey. The results of the survey will be used for a new product proposal in Unit 8.

Task: Use the following framework to outline your questionnaire. To fill in the blanks, you should apply what you have learned in the previous activities of Unit 7. And you may also need to refer to Unit 6 Activity 6 for more relevant information.

A. Content

    1. Introduction

        Purpose 1: surveying the attitudes towards the design

Purpose 2: surveying the attitudes towards the prototype's name

Purpose 3: surveying the attitudes towards the main characteristics (selling points)

Purpose 4: probing into the advantages over the competitors

Purpose 5: profiling the target customers

Purpose 6: surveying the attitudes towards the pricing strategies

Purpose 7: surveying the attitudes towards the sales channels (possible outlets)

2. The items for biographic information (to profile respondents):

   age range; 1) _____

3. Screening/filtering items (to classify respondents)

   Whether encountered the problem that the product is designed to solve;

   2) _____

4. The main items:

   The items addressing Purpose 1: look, size, color, etc.;

   The items addressing Purpose 2: like, dislike, be indifferent;

   The items addressing Purpose 3:

   waterproof; 3) _____

   The items addressing Purpose 4:

   waterproof; 4) _____

   The items addressing Purpose 5:

   fashion-conscious; 5) _____

   The items addressing Purpose 6:

   free gift; 6) _____

   The items addressing Purpose 7:

   supermarkets; 7) _____

B. Distribution

   Email; 8) _____

 **Section IV** *Drafting*

Activity 9 Writing the Introduction

Read the following Knowledge Notes about the essentials of the introduction section of a questionnaire and then complete the tasks that follow.

> **Knowledge Notes**
>
> When drafting a questionnaire, we need to think about what information should be included in each section. In particular, the introduction section usually contains information you want the respondents to know, for example, the significance, purpose, and even the time to finish the questionnaire. It may also state the requirements of filling in the questionnaire, explain some key terms and guarantee confidentiality. However, you don't have to include all of the information in your own questionnaire introduction.

Task 1: Analyze the two examples below and pick up the words or phrases from the box below to label the purposes of the sentences in the examples.

Example 1:

> Thank you for shopping at the NewStar Mall. We're conducting a short survey to find out about your shopping experience and what we may do to improve our service. Please complete the questionnaire and send it back to survey@newstar.com. Customers who complete the questionnaire will get a $10 voucher.

- The second sentence states the purpose of the questionnaire.
- The third sentence states the 1) _____.
- The last sentence is about 2) _____.

Unit 7　Conducting a Market Survey

Example 2:

> The Students Association is proposing a new supermarket on campus and would like to ask about your opinions. It will take only about three minutes to complete the questionnaire. Your feedback will be used to help decide the future direction of our campus' food choice. Please select only one answer unless otherwise specified. Thanks very much!

The second sentence states the 3) _____.

The last sentence states the 4) _____.

gratitude	time to finish the questionnaire
requirements of filling in the questionnaire	incentive

Task 2: Write down your group's questionnaire introduction for the market survey in Activity 8.

_____
_____
_____
_____
_____

Activity 10　Writing the Items

Read the following excerpt of a passage about some general rules for writing questionnaire items and then complete the tasks that follow.

Task 1: All the headings of the excerpt have been taken out and put in the box below. Put the headings back into the blanks above each paragraph. Then write your own questionnaire items for the market survey you are working on.

1) _____

　Make sure every respondent is able to answer the questions in your questionnaire—even if the question isn't relevant to them. Including an "other" or "none of the above" or "never" answer option can help you achieve this.

165

2) _____

There should be no overlaps in answer options (e.g., age ranges 20–30 and 30–40 both have 30 in them).

3) _____

Short, simple sentences are generally less confusing and ambiguous than long, complex ones.

4) _____

Do not ask for more than one piece of information at a time. Otherwise, it is unclear which one the respondents are answering (e.g., Please rate the lecture in terms of its content and presentation.)

5) _____

Make sure the items are precise. For example, items may become ambiguous because a word or term may have different meanings. Also, respondents may feel hard to answer the question that fails to specify a frame of reference. (e.g., How many books have you borrowed from the library?)

6) _____

Negatives can be confusing and difficult to understand and therefore, should be avoided. (e.g., Sentence A, "Small group teaching should continue", is more straightforward and clearer than Sentence B, "Small group teaching should not be abolished".)

A) Use Short and Simple Sentences
B) Ask for Only One Piece of Information at a Time
C) Avoid Negatives If Possible
D) Ask Precise Questions
E) The Answer Options Must Be Mutually Exclusive
F) Give Your Respondents All the Possible Options

Task 2: Write out all your group's questionnaire items based on the outline in Activity 8.

Unit **7** Conducting a Market Survey

Section V *Reflection*

Activity **11** Improving Bad Items

Sometimes there are a few bad items in a questionnaire. You should find them out and improve them.

Task: Revise the following bad items based on the rules of writing questionnaire items listed in Activity 10. The first item has been analyzed and revised as an example for your reference.

Questions	Analysis and Revision
What's your age? A. 20–30. B. 31–40. C. 41–50.	This example violates rule F), because the participant may be under 20. It can be revised by adding one option: D. None of the above.
How often do you visit our restaurant? A. Once. B. Twice. C. Three times and more. D. None of the above.	
How much time do you play a gamepad per week in the last two months? A. 0–2h. B. 2–6h. C. 6–10h. D. More than 10h.	
Please rate the gamepad's functions regarding its waterproof quality and 40-hour battery life. 1 2 3 4 5	

(Continued)

Questions	Analysis and Revision
The online class should not be cancelled. A. Strongly agree. B. Somewhat agree. C. Neither agree nor disagree. D. Somewhat disagree. E. Strongly disagree.	

Activity 12 Adding Red Herring Questions

A well-designed questionnaire does not guarantee that all the responses can be used for further analysis. The invalid responses must be selected out after their collection. Read a passage about quality control of the questionnaire responses and complete the task that follows.

It is necessary to take some quality control measures to ensure that the responses are suitable for analysis. For instance, incomplete responses, responses with contradictory or straight-lining answers are considered invalid, and therefore should be "cleaned" before analysis. To reduce the invalid responses, it is also a common practice to incorporate a questionnaire item containing a fake option among a set of valid ones (See Sample 2, Item 5 on the next page) to check if the respondent has paid attention. This type of question is called the red herring question.

Task: You are provided with some background information of a company's market survey below. Read the information and two samples of responses with their answer options circled by the respondents. Then discuss with a partner why the two example responses are invalid. You can use the hints in the following table for help.

SGC is a company that has developed three learning apps: Vocab Link, Conversation Link and Translation Link. Recently, SGC has conducted a market survey using online questionnaires to gain feedback from their existing customers, the university students in China. After launching the survey for two months, SGC is now running an initial data analysis to filter out the invalid responses and to see if they have obtained sufficient responses.

Unit 7 Conducting a Market Survey

Example 1:

... 1. Your gender: 　A. Male.　　B. Female. ✓ 2. Which university are you studying at? 　[　　　　　　　　　　] 3. Where is your university located? 　A. East.　　　B. South. 　C. West.　　　D. North. ✓ ... 15. The app is user-friendly. 　　　1　2　3　④　5 ...	Hint 1: There is one problem in relation to Item 2. 1) _____ _____ _____ _____ _____

Example 2:

... 1. Your gender: 　A. Male.　　B. Female. ✓ 2. Which university are you studying at? 　[　Chongqing University　] 3. Where is your university located? 　A. East.　　　B. South. 　C. West. ✓　　D. North. 4. Do you use any SGC learning apps? 　A. Yes.　　　B. No. ✓ 5. What SGC apps have you used? 　A. Vocab Link. 　B. Conversation Link. ✓ 　C. Translation Link. ✓ 　D. Talk Link. ✓ ... 15. The app is user-friendly. 　　　1　2　3　4　⑤ ...	Hint 2: There are two problems in relation to Items 4 and 5. 2) _____ _____ _____ _____ _____

Activity 13 Commenting on a Sample Questionnaire and Revising Yours

Study a sample questionnaire based on Activity 8 and complete the tasks that follow.

Task 1: Comment on the strengths and weaknesses of the following sample according to the reflection questions offered below.

Survey on the Prototype Product—Magic Gloves

We have designed a new product named Magic Gloves, and we wish to know your thoughts about it. There are 14 items in the questionnaire, which will take about 5 minutes to complete. Thank you for your support!

① Your gender:

    A. Man.

    B. Woman.

② How much do you spend on clothing each month?

    A. 200 yuan or less.

    B. 200–400 yuan.

    C. 400–600 yuan.

    D. 600–800 yuan.

    E. More than 800 yuan.

③ How often do you use gloves in winter?

    1 2 3 4 5

④ How much do you value keeping your winter gloves warm?

    1 2 3 4 5

⑤ How much importance do you attach to the light, thin and comfortable quality of the product and the wearable experience?

    1 2 3 4 5

⑥ The degree of importance you attach to the personalized design of the

Unit 7 Conducting a Market Survey

product (such as appearance, color variability, etc.) is

1 2 3 4 5

⑦ Indicate the level of importance you attach to wearing something that does not affect the experience of other activities (such as using a mobile phone).

1 2 3 4 5

⑧ How important do you think glove durability is?

1 2 3 4 5

⑨ How much importance do you attach to the shape of the glove (whether it is variable)?

1 2 3 4 5

⑩ The product price you can accept is

A. under 20 yuan.

B. 20–50 yuan.

C. 50–80 yuan.

D. 80–100 yuan.

E. 100 yuan or more.

⑪ Do you think the product commercial "Are you still choosing between staying warm in winter and using your phone? Try this." is attractive?

A. Yes.

B. No.

C. So so.

⑫ Would you like to try this product?

A. Yes.

B. No.

⑬ Do you think there is anything that appeals to you about our products?

_____

_____

⑭ Do you have any suggestions for improving our products?

_____

_____

Reflection Questions:

1) Has this questionnaire achieved all the purposes listed in Activity 8?
2) Does this questionnaire include all the necessary sections?
3) Will this questionnaire be improved by adding any other sections?
4) Does the introduction tell the respondents all the information needed?
5) Are the questionnaire items clear, concise and easy to understand?
6) Do the questionnaire items ask for one piece of information at a time?
7) Are there any negative questionnaire items?
8) Are the questionnaire items precise enough?
9) Are the questionnaire items mutually exclusive?
10) Do the questionnaire items give the respondents all the possible options?
11) Does the questionnaire contain any red herring questions?

Task 2: Revise your group's questionnaire completed in Activity 10.

Activity 14 Doing a Peer Review

Ask your classmates to give you feedback on your group's questionnaire revised in Activity 13. They need to follow the checklist below to evaluate the questionnaire.

Questions	Answers
Does the questionnaire cover all the purposes?	Yes ☐ No ☐
Does the questionnaire include all the necessary sections?	Yes ☐ No ☐
Can the questionnaire be improved by adding any other sections?	Yes ☐ No ☐

(Continued)

Questions	Answers
Does the introduction tell the respondents all the information needed?	Yes ☐ No ☐
Are the questionnaire items clear, concise and easy to understand?	Yes ☐ No ☐
Do the questionnaire items ask for one piece of information at a time?	Yes ☐ No ☐
Are there any negative questionnaire items?	Yes ☐ No ☐
Are the questionnaire items precise enough?	Yes ☐ No ☐
Are the questionnaire items mutually exclusive?	Yes ☐ No ☐
Do the questionnaire items give the respondents all the possible options?	Yes ☐ No ☐
Does the questionnaire contain any red herring questions?	Yes ☐ No ☐

Section VI *Exposition*

Activity 15 Showing the Survey Results

After the valid responses are analyzed, the survey is usually closed with a presentation about its results. Some students of your group need to hold a meeting to present your survey results assigned in Unit 6 Activity 16. Before you start the meeting you should review the rubric of that activity and prepare visual aids for the presentation. A picture is worth a thousand words! Therefore, it is critical to use graphs and charts to show the survey results in presentations. Nevertheless, there are several types of graphs and charts, which may fit into different situations.

Task 1: Match the four introductions below with the corresponding graphs and charts.

Introductions	Visual Types
It shows the breakup of a whole into different parts (answer options). Therefore, it is often used to compare the parts. However, too many answer options can make it messy. 1) This is about _____.	A) Bar Chart
It is the most popular way to display and compare categorical data (the bars) through the numeric values (the heights or lengths). The bars can be plotted vertically or horizontally. 2) This is about _____.	B) Word Cloud
It is usually used to show how results change over a specified time interval by tracking the trends—the ups and downs. Moreover, the same graph can contain several data series, which is useful for comparing trends. 3) This is about _____.	C) Line Graph
It is a visual presentation of words, also known as tag cloud. It is usually used to analyse open-ended questions. The size of a word indicates its importance, for example, the frequency it appears in texts. 4) This is about _____.	D) Pie Chart

Task 2: When using a graph or chart to present the survey results, you should make sure it is complete, clear and readable. Moreover, remember that you are showing the results rather than the raw data. Look at the following graphs and charts and some sentences to describe their problems. Fill in the blanks with the words or phrases in the box below to make the sentences complete.

Unit 7 Conducting a Market Survey

1) Question: What characteristics should a phone case have?

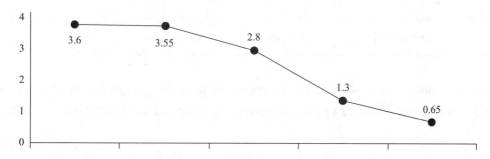

This line graph is not (1) _____, missing the x-axis (horizontal) values.

2) Question: Which advantages of the raincoats do you like?

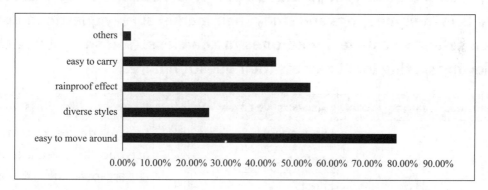

This bar chart is not (2) _____, almost impossible to read the percentage.

3) Question: Do you have any suggestions to improve the product's functionality?

1	More advertising	16	No
2	No	17	More intelligent
3	No	18	More on-line advertising
4	No	19	No
5	Free samples to try out	20	Easy to carry
6	No	21	No
7	No	22	No
8	Better insulation	23	No
9	No	24	No
10	Security matters most	25	No
11	No	26	No
12	No	27	Easy to carry
13	No	28	No
14	No	29	No
15	No	30	More positive adversiting

This is the (3) _____. You can improve it by using (4) _____.

| word cloud | complete | raw data | clear |

Task 3: Your group can hold a meeting now and a peer-review group will observe your group meeting and evaluate your performance (See the rubric of Unit 6 Activity 16).

Activity 16 Assessing the Unit Project

Watch all the other groups' videotaped presentations on their survey results in their meetings and study their market survey questionnaires. Then select 3 best-designed ones in the class. You should use the following scoring tool to assess their questionnaires.

Numbers	Names	Total	Aspects	Scores	Weights	Specifications
1			Language		20%	**Language** refers to the accuracy in language use and appropriateness of word choice. **Content** concerns the overall structure, the item types, the clarity, preciseness and the informative quality of the questionnaire. **Effects** mean to what extent the questionnaire items are tailored to the purposes of the survey and can guarantee high response reliability and validity.
1			Content		40%	
1			Effects		40%	
2			Language		20%	
2			Content		40%	
2			Effects		40%	
3			Language		20%	
3			Content		40%	
3			Effects		40%	
4			Language		20%	
4			Content		40%	
4			Effects		40%	
5			Language		20%	
5			Content		40%	
5			Effects		40%	

Unit 7 Conducting a Market Survey

Section VII *Wrap-Up*

Activity 17 Conducting Self-Evaluation

Use the following scale to self-evaluate your knowledge about conducting a market survey and how well you have done in learning this unit. Four in the right column means you totally agree with each statement on the left, while zero means you totally disagree with it.

Statements	Degree of Agreement
I have known the requirements for the unit project fully.	0 1 2 3 4
I can use the key terms in the market survey.	0 1 2 3 4
I am aware of the 5 basic parts of a questionnaire.	0 1 2 3 4
I can distribute the questionnaires to the target audience.	0 1 2 3 4
I can sample adequate respondents for the survey.	0 1 2 3 4
I can contain appropriate questionnaire items for different surveying purposes.	0 1 2 3 4
I can include all the necessary information in my introduction part.	0 1 2 3 4
I have mastered the rules for writing questionnaire items.	0 1 2 3 4
I have used some red herring questions in the questionnaire for quality control.	0 1 2 3 4
I can present the survey results with appropriate graphs and charts as visual aids for presentations.	0 1 2 3 4
I have improved my writing skills in this unit.	0 1 2 3 4

Unit 8

Writing a New Product Proposal

商务职场沟通英语

Section 1 Warm-Up

Activity 1 Initiating the Unit

Your group has designed a prototype product in Unit 6 and has conducted a market survey on the prototype in Unit 7. If you want to bring this new product into a specific market, what will you do next?

Task: Choose a possible option from the list below or offer your own answer to the above question. Then share your reasons with a partner or in the class.

1) Write an email to the project manager and persuade him or her to support the launch.

2) Call the project manager and explain why your business needs to launch the product.

3) Lobby an angel investor to provide your group with finance for the product launch.

4) Give suggestions to the project manager in writing to present why and when to launch the product.

Activity 2 Understanding the Key Concept

Michael is a project manager of Allizon, an international insurance company. When having a business trip with his boss John, Michael puts forward a new idea of sponsoring an online debate show as an advertising campaign strategy for their new insurance product. Read the conversation in pairs and complete the task that follows.

John: Hi, Michael. You look smart.

Michael: Yah, thank you, John. I have a good morning today.

John: Oh, What's going on?

Michael: I had a short meeting with my team, trying to work out the way of launching

Unit 8 Writing a New Product Proposal

our new product of Job Entry Insurance.

John: Good. Have you gotten any idea?

Michael: Well, I can't tell you in detail now. We found our way through brainstorming, and our agreed idea is to sponsor an online debate show attracting excellent college graduates all over the country.

John: Interesting! What are the key reasons?

Michael: We think that the new product is designed for college job-hunters, and the graduates are the right potential customers.

John: Sounds nice. But how can you make sure whether your potential customers like the new product or not?

Michael: Good question! We make them like it by debating!

John: Debate for what? How?

Michael: We'll first deliver commercials with catchy slogans that define the core values of our new product. Then we sponsor a well-known job-hunting website to webcast the debates live and offer the debaters topics adapted from or related to our slogans. As a number of debaters are arguing about the topics, they show their talents to the audience and the headhunters, and increase traffic to the website. This will be our opportunity to attract the potential customers and promote the awareness of our new product. And finally, we can launch it after the final debate with a relatively low cost.

John: Brilliant! I wish I can read your **proposal** of the debate show very soon.

Task: Explain what a proposal is in your own words.

_____

_____

You can check the reference here.

Knowledge Notes

A proposal is a professionally written document that either persuades the recipient to agree with the proposed way of addressing a problem or issue, or gets the reader to act on the suggestion. There are many business situations for which a proposal is needed: to get a new client, to get funding for a project, to troubleshoot a problem in a business, to provide a service, to bring a new product into the market, etc.

Section II Pre-writing

Activity 3 Distinguishing Proposals from Plans

Read a passage about the differences between proposals and plans. Then complete the task that follows.

Proposal and Plan, What Are the Differences?

A proposal, by definition, is a report that offers a solution to a problem, or a course of action in response to a specific need. A plan, however, is a document of the steps to achieve a goal with details of resources and timing. Sounds similar, right? Take business proposals and business plans as an example. They are two different kinds of documents in terms of both purposes and functions. In general, business plans specify how a business intends to realize its objectives and goals, while business proposals attempt to sell a business entity's product or service to a prospective client.

Business plans state a company's grand vision and are naturally tactical. They are written with a primary purpose of making potential investors interested in a company. They usually include description of the realistically achievable business goals, the planned scope of business, the details of core competitiveness, branding strategy, financial goals and other factors that can demonstrate the comprehensive strengths of a business.

Business proposals, in contrast, present a roadmap for undertaking a specific project or marketing a profitable product. They are intended to entice target investors to finance the suggested project or to convince the management to offer financial support. Business proposal writers should provide the readers with appealing reasons and feasible actions to get the approval for their desired support. A business proposal usually consists of executive summary, description of the product or service, market analysis, marketing strategy, operating plan, financial analysis, team management, risk analysis, etc.

Task: Study a graphic of a writing process and discuss with your partner whether the writing process is related to a business proposal or a business plan.

Unit 8 Writing a New Product Proposal

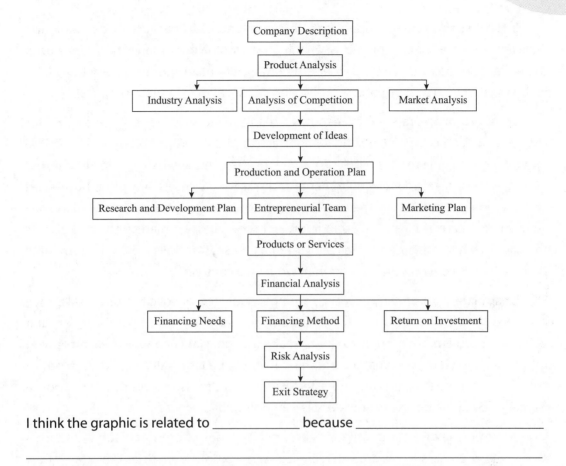

I think the graphic is related to _____ because _____
_____

Activity 4 Understanding the Basic Categories of Proposals

Read a passage about the four categories of proposals and complete the task that follows.

The Four Categories of Proposals

There are four categories of proposals, namely external proposal, internal proposal, solicited proposal and unsolicited proposal.

External proposals are written and sent out to an audience that is outside of your organization. A typical example is the independent consultant proposing to do a project for another firm. Since these are external documents, they are usually formal in nature.

Internal proposals are opposite to external proposals because of the audience. They are written to pitch a project or an initiative within your organization. Since both the writer and the reader work in the same organization, it is not necessary to include certain sections (such as corporate profile and qualifications) in these proposals.

Solicited proposals are in response to a request for proposals (or an RFP for short). Typically, a company looking for contractors to do a project often uses an RFP to find the right people for the project. That means the company issues a document that describes the project and its requirements and asks for proposals. Any other businesses or individuals interested in the project would then write a proposal in which they summarize their qualifications, arrange project schedules, estimate costs, and discuss their approach to the project. The recipient of all these proposals would then evaluate them, select the best candidate, and then work up a contract.

Unsolicited proposals, however, are not requested or solicited proposals. They can be submitted by subordinates to superordinates. You may initiate a proposal if you see a problem or an opportunity to make a beneficial change. For example, you may explain to your boss what a great thing it would be to install a new technology in the office; your boss might get interested and ask you to write a proposal to report a formal study of the necessity and feasibility of doing that.

Within those four basic categories are specific types of proposals submitted for a variety of purposes, such as project, technical, sales, product, financial, grant (a request for funding) proposals, etc. Therefore, the components of one type of proposal are very likely to differ from those of another. When you read a hundred proposals you may find no two are identical. On the other side of the coin, however, writing a strong proposal without a uniformed format can be a chance for you to win other rival proposals with shining ideas and sound reasoning.

Task: Study the following situations and consider what category of proposal should be adopted.

1) Your manager asks you to submit a funding proposal for your project research.

2) Your manager assigns you a project cooperation proposal based on an RFP.

3) Your team decides to submit a product repositioning proposal to your company's CEO.

4) Your manager assigns you to write an investment proposal to a group of potential investors.

Section III *Planning*

Activity 5 Understanding a New Product Proposal

A new product proposal is a specific type of proposal that provides a constructive statement and comprehensive analysis to convince clients or the management to approve the initiation of a new product development project. It is the target document you need to write before you can approach your project manager with the reasons for launching the new product you have designed in Unit 6 and surveyed in Unit 7. Therefore, what you should do first is to build specific awareness of what kind of new product proposal you actually need.

Task: Hold a group discussion to brainstorm the basics of the new product proposal you need, such as the purpose it will serve, the specific objectives it needs to achieve, the audience it will be sent to, etc. Then share your ideas with the other groups in your class. You may also consider the questions below to guide yourself to understand the proposal better.

1) Who will be the audience of the proposal?
2) Is the proposal internal or external?
3) Is the proposal solicited or unsolicited?
4) Is the primary purpose of the proposal explaining why to develop and launch the new product or presenting how to launch it?
5) What persuasive materials do you have to appeal to your project manager?
6) Do you explain to the reader(s) why you design the new product?
7) Do you describe the selling points of the new product in the proposal?
8) Do you report an analysis about the company's strengths, weaknesses, opportunities, and threats (SWOT)?
9) Do you summarize the market analysis concerning the size of the market, the

target customer profile, the rivalry, the advantages over the competitors, etc.?

10) Do you need substantial data to support the above analyses?

11) Do you state how to launch the new product in the market, including pricing, advertising, packaging, endorsement, outlets, etc.?

12) Do you propose the management team and their key roles?

13) Do you need a plan to deal with the potential risks?

14) Do you submit a timeline and budget for the product launch?

15) Do you estimate revenue streams from the product sales?

Activity 6 Familiarizing Yourself with Section Headings

A proposal consists of a number of sections (for short proposals) or chapters (for long proposals) named with headings. Before you can write a proposal you need to know the meanings of different headings.

Task: The section headings listed below are the basic components of a specific new product proposal. Match these headings on the left with their meanings on the right.

Section Headings	Meanings
1) Executive Summary 2) Product Description 3) Target Customers 4) Market Analysis 5) Product Launch 6) Financials 7) Risk and Avoidance 8) Budget 9) Timeline 10) Recommendations	A) A chronological order of planned dates, events, or important actions to do the project B) An estimate of sales targets, revenue streams and/or an outline of EBIT (Earnings Before Interest and Taxes) analysis C) A detailed SWOT analysis that assesses the conditions that affect a marketplace D) An overview that summarizes the key points of the proposal for the reader E) A profile of a specific group of people identified as most likely to purchase the target product F) A short part about other call-to-actions that haven't been written in the previous sections

Unit 8 Writing a New Product Proposal

(Continued)

Section Headings	Meanings
	G) A plan that details the efforts to debut a new product to the market and make it available
	H) An introduction that describes the features and benefits of a product
	I) A list of estimated costs requested to complete a business activity or project
	J) An examination of potential negative impacts that may harm a business initiative or project and the possible solutions

Activity 7 Analyzing an Outline

To make some changes to the present dull sales, Ann House, a property agency, calls for creative proposals from its staff. Sam, a sales executive, has proposed a short-term sightseeing treasure hunt for tourists to attract the target customers. A sightseeing treasure hunt is a game in which the enrolled tourists are grouped to compete for the first finders of one to many hidden objects or the first achievers of a series of assigned tasks. As a result, the winning group is usually awarded a sum of money or an expensive prize.

Task: Study Sam's proposal outline and answer the questions that follow.

A Product Marketing Proposal

Section 1 Executive Summary

    1.1 The problem to be solved: the dull property sales in the coastal districts since last year

    1.2 The goal: to increase house sales in the coastal districts by attracting the potential customers, especially elderly tourists

    1.3 The research: We have done a market survey and found that many migrant elderly people enjoy having a short-term tour in the coastal districts in autumn and winter, which is a good chance for us to promote our estates and properties.

1.4 The strategy: short-term sightseeing treasure hunt

1.5 The solution: We mean to outsource the treasure hunt to a reliable travel agency and provide venues (our properties on sale) for the events. We can provide the target customers with unforgettable tours to experience our property equipment, environment and management during the treasure hunt tours. Having witnessed and experienced the high quality and high value-added services we have demonstrated and offered, the target customers, in return, will be more likely to buy our estates and properties.

1.6 Team: Staff from both Ann House and the travel agency will work together to plan the events.

Section 2 Customers Analysis

2.1 The potential customers: people, especially the elders who like beautiful sea beach scenery and prefer to live in coastal residential areas

2.2 The target customers: After segmenting the market, we have found the target customers are migrant elderly couples who can afford well-furnished houses or apartments in coastal neighborhoods in autumn and winter.

Section 3 Market Analysis

3.1 Strengths: Our properties have good location, great convenience for public transport and shopping and well-furnished sea-view rooms.

3.2 Weaknesses: The target customers often complain about our properties' high price and long distance away from local medical resources.

3.3 Opportunities: There is an increasing market demand for high-end houses or apartments in the coastal districts, especially with customizable housework and medical services.

3.4 Threats: The local housing market will soon be saturated with an overheated house supply in recent months and house prices keep rising as a consequence of the soaring construction costs.

    3.5 Avoidance: to attract the target customers with desirable residential equipment and environment and to provide high value-added property management and medical and nursing services

Section 4 Marketing Strategy

    4.1 The reasons for adopting the strategy: The events of a sightseeing treasure hunt can provide the target customers with exciting tours in our properties on sale, which naturally and authentically demonstrates our equipment, environment and property management to the target customers and can eventually influence their purchases from us.

    4.2 The advantages over the rivalry: None of our competitors has ever adopted a sightseeing treasure hunt to market estates and properties. Our strategy is more approachable to customers compared with other marketing strategies.

Section 5 Marketing Plan

    5.1 The dates: every weekend from this October to December

    5.2 The venues: the selected houses and apartments on sale

    5.3 The moves: At first, find a travel agency. Next, entrust the sightseeing treasure hunt to the travel agency and communicate our requests to them. And then, select high-quality estates and properties as the venues for the events. Finally, award the winning treasure hunters with attractive discounts on house prices or bonuses and pitch for purchases.

Section 6 Budget

It depends on the scale of the treasure hunts, the number of customers and the commission requested by the travel agency.

Section 7 Timeline

Will be displayed in the proposal

Section 8 Recommendations

Will be stated in the proposal

1) What does Sam propose in his outline?
   _____
   _____

2) Why does he intend to do that?
   _____
   _____

3) What has been done before he outlines his proposal?
   _____
   _____

4) What is the advantage of the proposed marketing strategy?
   _____
   _____

5) What are the specific actions that Sam plans to take?
   _____
   _____

6) Do you think the outline includes all the key components it needs? Why or why not?
   _____
   _____

7) What improvement does this outline need?
   _____
   _____

Activity 8 Drawing Your Own Outline

Work in groups to draw your own outline for the new product proposal you have discussed in Activity 5. You can imitate the outline demonstrated in Activity 7 and assign one section or two to every

group member. Then assemble all the sections into a complete outline before the deadline. Finally, you should consult your teacher about the outline for feedback and revise it before you proceed to the next activity.

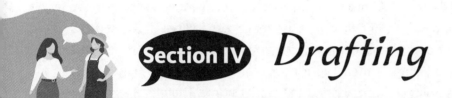

Section IV Drafting

Activity 9 Understanding the Guidelines

Despite the fact that every proposal is unique, there are still some rules that proposal writers should follow to increase the acceptance rate. Read a passage about the guidelines for proposal writing and complete the task that follows.

The Guidelines for Proposal Writing

Normally, proposal writing is considered to be difficult because of the disproportion between the high consumption of your time and energy and the low acceptance rate. It may be the first time you need to write a proposal. Therefore, you are highly recommended to get to know some common guidelines for proposal writing as follows.

1. Be prudent and committed. Before you write a proposal, consider whether you are in the right position to propose, how much energy and time you can offer, whether you have built credibility with the recipient and your boss, and what impact the proposed idea will have on the company's future. Once you set up your mind, just work hard.

2. Be direct and impressive. Begin your proposal with a problem-solution summary rather than a lot of background information. You will succeed in selling your ideas if you arouse the readers' interest and leave them with an impression.

3. Be prepared and rigorous. Don't give a response to an RFP until you understand the entire situation. Study the RFP carefully and understand the recipient's needs and requirements fully. If you don't, send them an inquiry.

4. Be realistic and objective. Don't exceed your responsibilities and capabilities to give any promises more than you can deliver. Think practically about your business scope, team size, current workload, financial status, profit expectation, etc. In addition, provide objective analyses and produce rational recommendations for the recipient.

5. Be specific and concise. In order to convince the recipient you should prove in the proposal that you have the knowledge, experience, capabilities and resources to get the proposed job done or to show how your approach can benefit the recipient. Being specific, however, doesn't mean your proposal contains more pages. In fact, you should get to the point without wasting the reader's time. Therefore, avoid excess words and meaningless information.

Task: You are provided with three couples of sentences, each with two different versions of expressions. Compare the two versions and decide which one is more appropriate according to the above passage.

Couple 1

Version A:	Given the fact that some puzzles in the treasure hunt are really difficult or unsuitable for the aged who are suffering memory loss, it may be necessary to consider an exit rule.
Version B:	If some puzzles in the treasure hunt are difficult or unsuitable for the aged, an exit rule will be needed.

1) I think Version _____ is more appropriate because _____

_____

Couple 2

Version A:	Our marketing strategy will be unveiled in Section 4. You are first provided with some information about our property agency and sales team.
Version B:	To promote our sales, we intend to adopt an innovative marketing strategy. The first few paragraphs allow you to see at a glance what we mean to offer the target customer.

2) I think Version _____ is more appropriate because _____

_____

Unit 8 Writing a New Product Proposal

Couple 3

> Version A: I think we need some changes in our marketing strategy. We should adopt a more innovative one, for example the treasure hunt.
>
> Version B: Research shows immersive experiences can promote real estate sales by 16%. Our innovative marketing strategy is to immerse the target customer not only in real environment but in real scenarios, for instance the treasure hunt.

3) I think Version _____ is more appropriate because _____
_____

Activity 10 Writing the Executive Summary

The section of executive summary highlights the basic elements of a proposal. Read a passage on the rules of writing the executive summary and complete the task that follows.

An executive summary is usually the first section of a business proposal. It summarizes a number of key points of the main part so that the reader can quickly become familiar with the proposal without having to read the entire document. It aims at helping managers to make decisions and is regarded as the most important part of a proposal.

The length of the executive summary varies. Some say one page is preferable and reader-friendly. For a 100-page proposal, however, the executive summary is normally up to 2 to 4 pages. Therefore, keep the executive summary concise and don't include the minute specifics.

If you want the readers to read the entire proposal, don't include cost or budget figures unless it is a strong selling point to do so. The reason is that the readers may stop reading if they think the figures are higher than what they have expected. Remember that you have only one chance to pitch your idea. If you do need to include the figures, follow immediately with the return value.

The executive summary should be written after the proposal has been completed. Only if you have all the specific information in advance can you summarize the most valuable points, stress the benefits, and give an impressive problem-solution description.

Task: Study a one-page sample executive summary in an external unsolicited proposal and identify the purpose of each paragraph. You are also provided with some phrases for your reference in the box below.

Pete's Pizzeria has been our favorite restaurant since the very first day we moved our offices to Toronto. The crispy-yet-fluffy crust is to die for, the sauce is otherworldly, and don't even get us started on that fresh buffalo mozzarella you use. Surely this isn't the first time you're hearing this, but we have a feeling that you don't hear it often enough. We noticed that you don't have much of a social media presence, which is unfortunate because we think that everyone in the city should be lining up to eat at Pete's Pizzeria.

If you weren't already aware, social media is one of the most effective ways to expand your reach and grow your business. Without it, you're leaving a giant, untapped pool of potential customers on the table and you risk losing existing, hungry customers to other restaurants that they follow. What you need is a social media marketing strategy to showcase your delicious restaurant in order to increase sales and customer loyalty.

Fortunately, uGrow can help. We'll leverage Instagram, Twitter, and TikTok to get your name out to millions of users. Here's how: First, we'll get you set up on each of the platforms and work with you to establish the Pete's Pizzeria brand and voice. Then, we'll take some stunning pictures of your food and write captions with trending hashtags. After that, we'll create a consistent content calendar and posting schedule to maximize engagement. And to top it all off, we'll manage all of the accounts to grow follower counts and increase traffic to your website. With this approach, we expect to increase your sales by 25% before year-end.

At uGrow, we specialize in helping small Toronto restaurants like Pete's Pizzeria reach their full potential and grow their business. We've worked with over 75 restaurants across the city and throughout the GTA, and every one of our clients saw an increase in sales within three months of us taking over their social media. We've had several posts go viral, which resulted in our clients' restaurants being completely sold out for the following weeks. All this to say: We love Pete's Pizzeria and want to help you get the attention you deserve.

If you're interested in increasing your sales by at least 25% by the end of the year, we can make it happen. This proposal goes into more detail on how exactly we plan to execute on your social media marketing strategy, and what you can expect once we start. Let's get Pete's Pizzeria trending.

Unit 8 Writing a New Product Proposal

| the call-to-action | the need | the evidence |
| the proposed solution | the opener | |

1) Paragraph 1 is _____.

2) Paragraph 2 is _____.

3) Paragraph 3 is _____.

4) Paragraph 4 is _____.

5) Paragraph 5 is _____.

Activity 11 Including Visuals

A successful proposal usually contains a variety of visuals that supply or clarify important points and make the proposal easy to comprehend. Some types of visuals, i.e., bar charts, word clouds, line graphs and pie charts, have been instructed in Unit 7 Activity 15. Complete the following tasks and learn some more types of visuals.

Task 1: Match the three introductions below with the corresponding visual types.

Introductions	Visual Types
It is now a popular visual type that is used to briefly and clearly present almost all kinds of information, including statistical data, knowledge, networks, patterns, trends, etc. 1) This is about _____.	A) Flowchart
It is a combination of tables and bar charts that illustrate a project schedule. It displays the start and finish dates of every activity of a project as well as its duration. 2) This is about _____.	B) Infographic

(Continued)

Introductions	Visual Types
It is a common visual type that shows a step-by-step approach to accomplish a task. It uses boxes of various kinds to sign the steps and connects the boxes with arrows to indicate their order. 3) This is about _____.	C) Gantt chart

Task 2: Hold a group discussion to answer the following questions that direct your visual use in your proposal. Write down your answers in the blanks below.

1) Where do you need visuals in your proposal?
   _____
   _____

2) What types of visuals do you include in your proposal?
   _____
   _____

3) If you are allowed to submit a proposal electronically, will you include videos and/or web links?
   _____
   _____

4) What color(s) do you think has a better persuasive effect? Why?
   _____
   _____

5) Do you need to give a title and number to each visual?
   _____
   _____

Unit 8 Writing a New Product Proposal

6) Where do you place the visuals, in certain sections or in the appendix?
_____
_____

7) Do you list your visuals in the list of illustrations on prefatory pages?
_____
_____

Activity 12 Completing the Unit Project

Now, work in groups to write up your entire proposal. Integrate all the knowledge and techniques you have learned in this unit when writing the proposal. Before you submit your proposal to your teacher, make sure you have also done all the things listed in the checklist below.

Questions	Answers
Does your proposal have a cover?	Yes ☐ No ☐
Does your proposal have a title page?	Yes ☐ No ☐
Does your proposal contain the table of contents?	Yes ☐ No ☐
Do you have the list of illustrations on prefatory pages?	Yes ☐ No ☐
Do you include a copy of the RFP in the prefatory part if necessary?	Yes ☐ No ☐
Do you offer footnotes wherever necessary?	Yes ☐ No ☐
Do you add appendix pages to your proposal?	Yes ☐ No ☐
Do you add page numbers to your proposal?	Yes ☐ No ☐
Have you already had your proposal proofread?	Yes ☐ No ☐
Have you converted your proposal into a PDF file?	Yes ☐ No ☐

Section V Reflection

Activity 13 Improving Your Language

If you want to stand out with a well-written proposal, improve your language. Read a passage about the rules of language use in proposals and complete the tasks that follow.

Setting Your Proposal Language Right

One of the major reasons for proposals getting rejected is language problems. There are several things you can do to improve the language of your proposal.

　　1. Choose the appropriate tone for the reader. Tone or tone of voice is the overall attitude you take and the general way you write in a proposal. Obviously, the tone of the proposal should be active and positive. Nevertheless, when it comes to whether it is formal or not, there isn't a single answer. If you're creating a proposal for the government or a company you have never known, you will have to be professional and formal. If the readers are from a firm with business connections with you or in your own organization, you can use less formal language. An effective way of being formal is to write in the third person.

　　2. Don't use fluff and weasel words. Fluff words are meaningless and unimportant to the readers; and weasel words are vague, ambiguous or misleading expressions that are used to intentionally avoid giving definite answers or making direct statements. Typical examples are modal verbs like "could", "might" (equals the saying of "cannot"); adjectives like "better", "improved" (doesn't say how much); adverbs like "maybe", "almost" (means haven't yet); quantifiers like "much", "plenty" (lacks definite figures); linking verbs like "seems", "appears" (sounds uncertain); and the like. Most readers will recognize sentences with the above words as meaningless or vague statements that merely leave your credibility and reliability questioned.

　　3. Use the readers' jargons. Jargons are special words or technical terms used by a particular group of people in the same profession or organization. Using jargons in

proposals is inevitable and it demonstrates your expertise. However, proposals should be easy to read and easy to understand. The way to tackle the dilemma depends on to whom the proposal will be sent. Don't fill your proposal with the internal company jargons that are difficult for the external readers to understand. Instead, use your readers' jargons. For example, keep ROI (return on investment) in your proposal, while replacing NOI (net operating income) with cash flow.

4. Avoid wordiness. When we take the readers' time, energy and attention span into consideration, redundancy or wordiness is the major enemy of proposal writers. One of the major problems that cause redundancy is filler words that fill up space in writing without adding real meaning. Clichés, for instance, are used when the writer can't think of something more accurate or original. In the sentence "For what it's worth, I will appreciate your support for our initiative.", "for what it's worth" is such a filler phrase that connotes the writer is not sure whether something he/she is about to say will be helpful or valued. To edit out the redundant words, you need to identify them. If you can't, have your proposal examined by well-experienced reviewers who will offer the proposal team recommendations for improvement and approaches to minimize potential risks.

Task 1: Re-read the executive summary in Activity 10 and answer some questions based on the rules instructed in the above passage.

1) Is the tone of voice in the executive summary formal or informal? How do you know it? Do you think it is appropriate to write in that tone? Why or why not?

   _____

   _____

2) Are there any fluff and weasel words in the executive summary? Give examples if there are some and explain why.

   _____

   _____

3) Are there any unfamiliar jargons for you in the executive summary? Give examples if there are some and replace them with the words you can understand.

   _____

   _____

4) Are there any redundant words or expressions in the executive summary? Identify them and improve the sentences.

_____

_____

Task 2: Work in groups to improve the language of your own proposal. You can also trade your proofreading job with another group in your class.

Activity 14 Doing a Peer Review

Work in groups to read the improved version of another group's new product proposal (See Activity 13) and give feedback to the writers. The readers should use the checklist below for help.

Questions	Answers
Is the document a new product proposal?	Yes ☐ No ☐
Is the purpose of the proposal to persuade the manager to launch the new product?	Yes ☐ No ☐
Is it an internal unsolicited proposal?	Yes ☐ No ☐
Does the proposal contain all the components it needs?	Yes ☐ No ☐
Does the proposal begin with a problem-solution executive summary?	Yes ☐ No ☐
Does the executive summary cover all the key points of the proposal?	Yes ☐ No ☐
Is the proposal easy to read and easy to understand?	Yes ☐ No ☐
Is the proposal concise?	Yes ☐ No ☐
Does the proposal give specific reasons for the launch?	Yes ☐ No ☐
Are the analyses in the proposal objective?	Yes ☐ No ☐
Are the recommendations in the proposal realistic?	Yes ☐ No ☐
Are the visuals in the proposal appropriate?	Yes ☐ No ☐
Does the proposal include a prefatory part?	Yes ☐ No ☐
Does the proposal include appendix pages?	Yes ☐ No ☐
Does the proposal have any language problems?	Yes ☐ No ☐
Does the proposal have a satisfactory persuasive effect?	Yes ☐ No ☐

Unit 8 Writing a New Product Proposal

Section VI *Exposition*

Activity 15 Revising Your Proposal

Work in groups to revise your proposal for the second time based on your self-reflection in Activity 13 and the readers' feedback in Activity 14. Print out your revised version and submit it to your teacher.

Activity 16 Assessing the Unit Project

Read all the other groups' proposals and select two best-written ones in your class. You should use the following scoring table to assess their proposals.

Numbers	Names	Total	Aspects	Scores	Weights	Specifications
1			Language		30%	**Language** refers to the accuracy in language use, appropriateness of tone, and avoidance of fluff, weasel words, internal jargons and redundancy. **Content** concerns the overall structure, the key components, the specific, concise, realistic, objective, reader-friendly qualities of writing, and the clarity. **Effects** mean to what extent the proposal achieves its purpose and can guarantee a high acceptance rate.
1			Content		40%	
1			Effects		30%	
2			Language		30%	
2			Content		40%	
2			Effects		30%	
3			Language		30%	
3			Content		40%	
3			Effects		30%	
4			Language		30%	
4			Content		40%	
4			Effects		30%	
5			Language		30%	
5			Content		40%	
5			Effects		30%	

Section VII Wrap-Up

Activity 17 Conducting Self-Evaluation

Use the following scale to self-evaluate your knowledge about writing a new product proposal and how well you have done in learning this unit. Four in the right column means you totally agree with each statement on the left, while zero means you totally disagree with it.

Statements	Degree of Agreement
I have known the requirements for the unit project fully.	0 1 2 3 4
I can identify the four basic categories of proposal.	0 1 2 3 4
I have clear awareness of what a new product proposal means.	0 1 2 3 4
I can outline a proposal before writing it.	0 1 2 3 4
I am aware of the basic rules of proposal writing.	0 1 2 3 4
I am aware of the basic rules for writing the executive summary.	0 1 2 3 4
I can use visuals properly in the proposal.	0 1 2 3 4
I can avoid major language problems of proposal writing.	0 1 2 3 4
I can add prefatory and appendix pages to the proposal.	0 1 2 3 4
I think our proposal has fulfilled its purpose.	0 1 2 3 4
I have improved my writing skills in this unit.	0 1 2 3 4

Appendix

Foundations of Speaking Delivery Skills

If you need to inform somebody of something or interact with others, which of the following two things will be a bigger challenge to you—preparing what you want to speak about or deciding how you speak? To most people, the delivering process makes them more likely to feel uneasy.

Delivery, by definition, refers to the way in which someone speaks. Any professionals consciously or subconsciously employ some delivery skills when engaging in business communication, be it answering job interview questions instructed in Unit 2, socializing to establish business connections instructed in Unit 4, giving business presentations instructed in Unit 5, or participating in business meetings instructed in Unit 6. Actually, professional delivery contributes a lot to making your speech a big success by helping you convey your points clearly, effectively, and in an attractive way. Though delivery differs from person to person, a general understanding of basic delivery skills is also necessary.

Normally, you can improve your delivery skills in the following two aspects.

1. Vocal skills

Different people have different vocal traits. Someone with a golden voice does have advantages in making a speech, but an undistinguished voice doesn't necessarily prevent you from being a good speaker. The skills of using voice mainly involve the following elements.

1) Volume

Making sure that you can be clearly heard should always be the first concern. A loud and powerful voice is necessary for a speaker, but it should be kept at an appropriate level. A good speaker should also be aware of the positions of different listeners, ensuring that the voice can reach every one of them. If you are equipped with a microphone, test it before the speech and keep a proper and flexible distance to it in the speech.

2) Pitch

The pitch refers to the highness of the voice. A monotonous voice usually counts as nothing but a lullaby to the audience. Conversely, inflection can be a good way to save both you and your audience, which can help show emotions and arouse echoes. Even though it is not suitable for you to show your feelings in some circumstances like a negotiation meeting, you can also use inflection to show your attitude and standpoint. In addition, when you are raising a question or trying to grasp some special attention, you can still resort to inflection, for example, raise the pitch when the key information appears.

3) Pace

Speaking speed varies a lot from individual to individual, but there are also some tips to follow. Firstly, you have to make sure that your audience can follow your talking easily instead of being desperate to catch up with you. Secondly, similar to the inflection of pitch, adjustment of the pace is also a necessity in delivery. It is advisable to slow down at some information that is important or hard to understand. Of course, you can also speed up if you want to create an atmosphere of urgency.

4) Pause

Mark Twain once said, "The right word may be effective, but no word was ever as effective as a rightly timed pause." Pause is intentionally made by the speaker to give the speech a nice rhythm, so those unnecessary pauses such as "um", "oh" and "let me see" resulting from nervousness or forgetting what you want to say are not what we need in the speech. When you are making a pause, make sure it will not break a thought unit, but you can use it after or before a thought unit to direct people's attention to the information you have conveyed or you are going to convey. Last but not least, pauses are always accompanied by inflection and eye contact.

2. Non-vocal skills

In a communication, be it a daily chat, a formal meeting or public speech, non-vocal skills also play a prominent role. Only by a collaboration of vocal skills and proper personal appearance, posture, facial expressions, eye contact, and gestures, can the communication be efficient and effective.

1) Personal appearance

Technically, personal appearance is not a delivery skill. But a good personal image of decent dressing, proper hair style and makeup can make the audience more willing to listen to you. Moreover, you especially need to pay attention to personal appearance in some formal situations, such as job interview, business meeting, etc.

2) Posture

Though you needn't pose as upright as soldiers, sitting or standing straight in a natural way is also extremely recommended in your delivery. When you stand, don't shift your weight between feet too frequently. No matter whether you sit or stand, don't shake your legs. Necessary turning and inclination to your audience can help keep you more connected with them.

3) Facial expressions

A poker-faced speaker is seldom a welcome one. You may not need a mobile or over-animated face, but don't be hesitant to show your facial expressions. A smile can show not only your friendliness but also your confidence and even professionalism. Meanwhile, solemn, sad, cheerful and other facial expressions are also helpful for you to convey your information.

4) Eye contact

Though people from different cultural backgrounds may have different habits of using eye contact, it is widely agreed that avoiding eye contact in a face-to-face or live communication will weaken its efficiency and effect. As the saying goes, the language world in eyes can be understood by people everywhere. As a speaker, what you need to do is just take the first step. If you are talking to only one person, just look at his or her eyes frequently and avoid staring which is considered to be rude. If you are speaking to a small audience, you can have eye contact with each of them briefly from time to time. If you are addressing a big audience, scanning and occasional eye contact with some people will help maintain the connection between you and the audience. It is worth noting that eye contact should be made throughout the communication process and should always appear together with your application of the vocal skills. Meanwhile, it is fairly reasonable to focus your eyes more on those who are expected to pay special attention to the very information you are conveying.

5) Gestures

Gestures refer to movements of parts of your body, especially your hands. Actually, there is not a fixed requirement of how to make gestures, but there are indeed some tips for you. Firstly, be spontaneous and natural. Secondly, make gestures in a moderate way lest they distract the audience. Thirdly, don't wring your hands or hide them in your pockets.

Practice makes perfect. Having known the above skills, you need to make yourself better and better at utilizing them in real situations. There are some additional suggestions for you. Firstly, make a good preparation for what you are going to say and try to make rehearsals if you have the chance. Secondly, pay attention to the reaction and feedback of your audience and adjust the way you talk. Thirdly, if you use slides or some materials while you are talking, don't rely on and stick to them too much in case you lose the connection with the audience.